THE FINAL CURTAIN

Chuck Smith

HARVEST HOUSE PUBLISHERS
Eugene, Oregon 97402

THE FINAL CURTAIN

Copyright © 1991 by Word for Today
Eugene, Oregon 97402

Library of Congress Cataloging-in-Publication Data

Smith, Chuck.
   The final curtain : prophecy's events leading to the Second
Coming / Chuck Smith.
   ISBN 0-89081-938-6
   1. Second Advent.   2. Bible—Prophecies.   I. Title.
BT886.S58   1991
236'.9—dc20   91-722
                                                     CIP

Printed in the United States of America.

Contents

Setting the Stage

Setting the Stage

We are living in extremely exciting days. It's as if we were backstage at a play feeling the drama and excitement just before the curtain rises for the final scene. The director is positioning all the players and seeing that the props are in order before he signals for the curtain to rise. This analogy is apt, for before our very eyes God is positioning nations and current events. The world is ready for the curtain to be lifted for the final act.

God is orchestrating the final events prior to the return of Jesus Christ. Have you ever stood dominoes on end in a long row? When you tip the first domino the whole line goes down in sequence. God is aligning world situations much as we would line up dominoes. He is getting ready to tip the first event which will trigger a series of actions ultimately climaxing in the Second Coming of Jesus Christ in power and great glory.

Before we begin to look at world events in light of Bible prophecy, let me emphasize one point. I have no intention of telling you the day that the Lord is coming for His Church. I don't know that day. Nobody knows that day or hour,[1] but the Bible does say, "Of the times and the seasons, brethren, you have no need that I write unto you. For you yourselves know perfectly that the day of the Lord so cometh as a thief in the night . . . but ye, brethren, are not in darkness, that that day should overtake you as a thief."[2]

God wants and expects us to be thoroughly aware of the times in which we live. To this end, He gave us many signs to help us recognize the time of His promised return.

1

Looking Back to Look Ahead

Daniel is one of the most fascinating books of prophecy in the Bible. Daniel, a young Hebrew, was captured by King Nebuchadnezzar in the first conquest of Israel by the Babylonians. His prophecies give us keen insights into the events that lead to Christ's return.

One night King Nebuchadnezzar had a nightmare that greatly troubled him. He awoke in the morning terrified by the dream but unable to remember it. The king was left with only a lingering aftereffect of horror. Feeling that his dream held a message of critical significance, Nebuchadnezzar called together all the wise men, astrologers, and soothsayers in the Babylonian kingdom and ordered them to explain the meaning. They asked him to recount his dream so that they could interpret it for him.

Nebuchadnezzar told them he could not recall the details of his nightmare, yet he threatened to cut off their heads if they could not interpret it for him. They could not believe the unreasonable demand the king made. They knew that they could not reveal the meaning of a dream that the king could not even remember. They realized their death was inevitable.

Arioch, the captain of the king's guard, told young Daniel of the danger he faced because of the king's decree. Daniel was being groomed as a counselor, so he too was to be executed. He asked the captain to tell the king that there is a God in heaven who knows all things, and that His servant Daniel, would reveal to the king his dream and what it meant. Arioch told Nebuchadnezzar of the young Hebrew captive who served a God who could answer the king's request.

Meanwhile Daniel went to his friends and told them to pray that God might reveal the king's dream to them. God was faithful and revealed the dream and its interpretation. Daniel was quickly brought before Nebuchadnezzar. The king said that he'd heard that this young man could tell him his dream and interpret its meaning.

Daniel answered, "No, I can't. But there is a God in heaven who knows all things. He knows what you dreamed and what it means, and He has revealed it to me." Then he continued, "The other night, O King Nebuchadnezzar, as you were lying on your bed, you were thinking of the power and greatness of your Babylonian kingdom. Then the thought came into your mind, 'What shall come to pass in the future? What will happen to my kingdom? How will the world end?' So God gave you a dream and has revealed to you what will take place in the last days.

"In your dream you saw a great image. It had a head of gold, breast and arms of silver, stomach and thighs of brass, legs of iron, and feet of iron and clay with ten toes. You watched the image until a stone not cut with hands hit the great image in its feet. The whole image crumbled and the stone grew into a mountain that filled the whole earth." At that moment Nebuchadnezzar recalled the dream that Daniel described and pressed him to explain what it meant.

Daniel explained, "You, O king, are the head of gold. God has given you a great and powerful kingdom which has extended throughout the civilized earth. After you, another kingdom shall rise that is inferior to you." In Daniel 8:20, this kingdom is identified as the Medo-Persian Empire which under Cyrus did indeed conquer Babylon. However, as the interpretation continued, this kingdom was also to be supplanted by the kingdom represented by the brass stomach, which in Daniel 8:21 is identified as Greece. This is a fascinating prophecy indeed, for at this time (approximately 600 B.C.) Greece was a small, almost unknown province in the western part of the world.

The kingdom of Greece was to be conquered by the kingdom represented by the iron legs which historically turned out to be the Roman Empire. Rome was as strong as iron, and it broke and subdued the world under its iron fist. So far these predictions have unfolded in an easily traceable historical sequence. But we are left with a prediction of a final world-dominating kingdom not specifically identified and not yet exercising its rule over the earth, for since the time of the Roman Empire there has not been a power that dominated the entire world.

From the description of its makeup as part iron and part clay, inasmuch as the iron represented imperial Rome, the final kingdom will be related to the Roman Empire. The fact that it is mixed with clay indicates that it will be weaker than iron alone. This could possibly signify a weak attempt at reviving imperial Rome. We are told that the ten toes represent ten kings that shall unite their power.

This prophecy could easily be embodied by the nations of Europe that are presently binding themselves together with economic treaties for the purpose of forming a United States of Europe or much more powerful version of the European Economic Community (EEC). Plans have been announced to remove all of the borders within the EEC nations at midnight, December 1992. A common European currency already exists and may supplant individual monetary systems by the end of the decade. We are just beginning to realize the awesome ramifications to world commerce when such an economic giant is created.

The exciting aspect of this whole prophecy to Bible believers is found in Daniel 2:44, where we are told that it is during the days of these kings that the God of heaven will come to establish His kingdom which shall never be destroyed. This Rock cut without human hands is Jesus Christ, who is coming again to establish God's everlasting kingdom.

When Nebuchadnezzar heard Daniel's interpretation of his dream, he acknowledged that indeed there was no god in all the world like the God of Daniel.[3]

Later though, Nebuchadnezzar defied the revelation of God and ordered a great image 90 feet high and made entirely of gold to be erected in the plain of Dura. By making it all gold, Nebuchadnezzar was declaring that no one would conquer his kingdom and that Babylon would stand forever. The king ordered all the people to bow down and worship this golden image. This is where the story of the three young Hebrew men, Shadrach, Meshach, and Abednego comes in. They refused to bow to the image and were cast into a burning furnace. There in the flames, a fourth man with the likeness of the Son of God joined them and protected them from being harmed by the fire.[4] The question arises, Where was Daniel at the time that his close buddies were going through this ordeal? We must assume that he either bowed down to the image (which is very unlikely) or that he was out of the country at the time. This story contains a fascinating analogy, for Scripture tells us that the Antichrist is going to set up an image in the last days and demand that mankind bow to it or be put to death.[5] The three Hebrews are a type of the 144,000 Jews that the Lord will seal to preserve them through this time of fiery judgment.[6] Daniel's absence may be a type of the Church which will be mysteriously gone during the Tribulation.

After this, Nebuchadnezzar went insane and lived and ate with the wild oxen in the fields. His hair grew long and covered his body like feathers, and his nails became like claws. He took total leave of his senses until seven seasons passed over him. It is unclear whether "seven seasons" refers to seven years or seven literal seasons, such as winter, spring, summer, and fall. Nebuchadnezzar could have been beside himself for 1¾ years or for seven whole years. Regardless of the length of his insanity, he remained in this condition long enough to know that the God in heaven lifts up and establishes kings and pulls down those whom He chooses. The king acknowledged the power of God until the end of his life.[7]

During the first year of King Belshazzar's reign, approximately 70 years after Nebuchadnezzar's dream, Daniel had a vision. He saw a lion with the wings of an eagle. It was devoured by a bear with three ribs in its mouth. The bear was destroyed by a leopard. This, in turn, was followed by a fierce animal that he couldn't really describe. It was terribly awesome and had ten horns. An eleventh horn rose up and destroyed three others. This horn then became a great power, speaking blasphemous things. In many ways, Daniel's vision paralleled Nebuchadnezzar's dream. The four animals in Daniel's vision represented the same world-governing empires as the metals of the image in Nebuchadnezzar's dream.

Looking at history, we can see that these prophecies of Daniel have been fulfilled. The Babylonian Empire (represented by the head of gold, or lion) was overthrown by the Medo-Persians (breast of silver, or bear), the Medo-Persian empire by the Greeks (stomach of brass, or leopard), and the Grecian empire by the Romans (legs of iron, or indescribable beast).[8]

The European Community

What relevance does this prophecy of successive empires hold for us today? As we look to current events, we see the formation of the European Economic Community, originally known as the Common Market. This is an organization of nations that have established treaties among themselves for commercial purposes. These nations admit that their economic treaties are only a prelude to future political and ultimately military alliances.

The original idea for the formation of the EEC came from a group of intellectuals known as the Club of Rome.

The confederacy of European nations is relevant to this discussion because each nation in the EEC was once a part of the old Roman Empire. This could be coincidence, but it does fit the Scripture without straining the text.

The EEC has increased to twelve member-nations at the present time, which provides a slight problem for those who see the ten toes as ten literal nations. However, some scholars believe that the number ten is merely a symbolic designation for an undetermined number of political entities. There are however, many other possible solutions. The latest maps of Europe list the nation north of France as Benelux. This is a combination of the three small nations of Belguim, the Netherlands, and Luxembourg. All are listed separately as member-nations of the Community. If they were recognized as one, there would then be ten nations corresponding to the ten toes. Other factors could also come into play such as nations dropping from the alliance. Daniel 7:8 tells us that an eleventh horn shall arise which will destroy three of the horns. This eleventh horn is identified as the Antichrist who will rise to rule over the world.

On December 31, 1992, the borders between the nations of the EEC will be removed and a common passport will be issued. This will be the official realization of the dream of the Club of Rome.

To be realistic, we do recognize a serious problem with the scenario. Western Europe can never rise as a world-dominating power as long as the Soviet Union exists as a major military threat to the European continent. The Soviets have been building a tremendous military arsenal and have positioned much of their might against Western Europe. As long as the USSR has such tremendous military capabilities, Soviet power prohibits Western Europe or the EEC from prevailing. Even though the nations of the EEC have a greater potential gross national product than the United States, and could conceivably become the greatest economic power in the world, they can never rise to world-governing stature as long as the Soviet Union overshadows them.

And yet this barrier seems to be falling. The whole Western world has been shocked by the events that took shape in 1990. The apparent collapse of Communism, the dismantling of the Berlin Wall, the reunification of Germany, and the liberalizing of Eastern Europe sent shock waves around the world. With the collapse of the Soviet economy, it would appear that God is removing this last obstacle.

As we will find out later, God has still other plans to reduce the military threat of Russia.

The Antichrist

Once God destroys the military power of the Eastern Bloc, the final world empire will be able to take control. From this confederacy of ten nations there shall arise the "horn"—a man of authority and power who will become the single most powerful leader in the history of the world. He is known in the Scriptures by various names such as "the beast," "the man of sin," and "the son of perdition," but he is commonly referred to as the Antichrist. He will oppose all that is in heaven and seek to exalt himself above God.[9]

The Antichrist will first come to public prominence with a successful peace program, and an entirely new commercial system.[10] He will work wonders with the world economy and will be known for the miraculous. People will stand in awe of him and hail him as the savior of the world. He will satisfy the world's tremendous desire for security. We already see the powerful peace movements that have risen among the nations of Europe. There are growing peace demonstrations all over the world; the stage is surely set for the emergence and acceptance of this scripturally described man of sin and his plan for universal peace.

There will be an apparently successful assassination attempt on his life but, miraculously, he will survive. As a result the Antichrist will lose the sight of his right eye and the use of one arm.[11] The Antichrist will then be involved in an event that will mark the beginning of the countdown of the last 1,290 days before the Lord of glory comes to establish His eternal kingdom. Jesus referred to this event as "the abomination that causes the desolation."[12] This same event is further described in Daniel 9. There we read that while Daniel was in prayer near the time of the evening oblation, the angel Gabriel appeared to him. He said to Daniel, "I am now come forth to give you skill and understanding. At the beginning of your supplications the commandment came forth, and I have come to show you; for you are greatly beloved: therefore, understand the matter, and consider the vision. Seventy weeks [or sevens] are determined upon your people and upon the holy city [Jerusalem], to finish the transgression, and to make an end of sins, and to make reconciliation for iniquity, and to bring in everlasting righteousness, and to seal up [to complete] the vision and prophecy, and to anoint the most Holy."[13] The word "week," which in Hebrew is *shabua*, means seven and refers to a week of years, or seven years.

Several events are spoken of here. "To finish the transgression . . . to make an end of sins . . . to make reconciliation for iniquity," these all belong in one category: They were all fulfilled in the first coming of Jesus Christ. "To bring in everlasting righteousness . . . to complete the visions and prophecy . . . to anoint the most Holy" have not yet been fulfilled.

They await their fulfillment when Jesus comes again.

Gabriel continued, "Know therefore and understand, that from the going forth of the commandment to restore and to build Jerusalem unto [the coming of] the Messiah the Prince shall be seven weeks, and threescore and two weeks [seven sevens and 62 sevens]: the street shall be built again, and the wall, even in troublous times. And after threescore and two weeks [62 sevens] shall Messiah be cut off, but not for himself [without receiving the kingdom]."[14] This is an amazing prophecy. For centuries the Jews had been waiting for their Messiah, and here God told Daniel the very day of His arrival.

According to the prophecy, the Messiah was to come 69 x 7 (or 483) years after the command went forth to restore and rebuild Jerusalem. Because Daniel was using the Babylonian calendar, which contained 360 days to the year, we must multiply 69 x 7 x 360, which equals 173,880 days. On March 14, 445 B.C., King Artaxerxes gave the command to Nehemiah to restore and rebuild Jerusalem.[15] Exactly 173,880 days later on April 6, 32 A.D., Jesus made His triumphant entry into Jerusalem riding on a donkey as was prophesied in Zechariah 9:9: "Rejoice greatly, O daughter of Zion; shout O daughter of Jerusalem: behold your King cometh unto you: He is just, and having salvation, lowly and riding upon an ass." Thus Jesus made His triumphant entry amid the shouts of His disciples who were actually quoting Psalm 118, one of the messianic Psalms. The section they were quoting (verses 24-26) begins with the declaration, "This is the day which the Lord hath made; we will rejoice and be glad in it." On that same day, as Jesus cried over Jerusalem, He said, "If you had known, even you, at least in this your day, the things which belong unto your peace! But now they are hid from your eyes."[16] This was the day the Messiah would come. God kept His promise. However, the Holy Spirit had predicted through Isaiah that He would be despised and rejected by men (Isaiah 53:3) and as the angel said to Daniel, "the Messiah will be cut off." In perfect fulfillment of these prophecies, Jesus was rejected, crucified, and cut off without receiving the kingdom.

The 69 sevens have thus been accounted for, but the angel said there are 70 sevens determined upon the nation Israel. The seventieth "week" of Daniel has not yet been fulfilled. The end of the seventieth seven will bring the completion of all the visions and prophecies, the most Holy place will be anointed, and Jesus will establish God's eternal, righteous kingdom.

Jesus Christ was cut off without receiving His kingdom. He did not bring in the age of everlasting righteousness, as is so evident today as we look around and see the world in which we live. The most Holy has not yet been anointed. Therefore, all of the prophecies in Daniel have not yet been fulfilled. We have yet to complete the seventieth seven-year period.

The angel continued to tell Daniel, "The prince [the false Messiah or Antichrist] that shall come . . . shall confirm the covenant with many for one week." In the midst of the week, or final seven-year period, he will break the covenant and set up the abomination which causes the desolation.[17]

When the disciples asked Jesus what the signs of the end of the world would be, He replied, "When ye therefore shall see the abomination of desolation, spoken of by Daniel the prophet, stand in the holy place, (whoso readeth, let him understand) then let them which be in Judea flee into the mountains, let him which is on the housetop not come down to take any thing out of his house, neither let him which is in the field return back to take his clothes."[18] The fact that Jesus referred to this event as future in His day and related it to the time of His Second Coming precludes any interpretation that would place the seventieth seven in past history.

What is the "abomination of desolation" that Daniel the prophet speaks about? The Antichrist will make a covenant with the nation Israel. As part of that covenant, he will grant the Israelites the right to rebuild the temple in Jerusalem and will promise to bring them peace. Then after $3\frac{1}{2}$ years the Antichrist will violate this agreement and cause the daily sacrifices and oblations to cease. He will stand in the holy place of the rebuilt temple and declare that he is God, and demand to be worshiped.[19] This is the abomination (a horribly disgusting act) that causes the desolation (the making of a holy place wretched). The word desolation also means "great agony or emptiness," and is used to refer to the Great Tribulation. At this point the eyes of the Jews will be opened and they will see that they have been deceived by the Antichrist. Many will then flee to sanctuary in southern Jordan. From that day it will be only 1,290 days until Jesus comes again in power and glory.

The beginning of 1991 saw an outbreak of war once again in the Middle East. This time a coalition of nations mustered against Iraq. Modern-day Iraq is the rough equivalent of the biblical nation of Babylon, making the many prophecies of the destruction of Babylon even more compelling. In Isaiah 13, the prophet declares, "The burden of Babylon which Isaiah the son of Amoz did see." In verse 4 he speaks of "the noise of a multitude in the mountains, like as of a great people; a tumultuous noise of the kingdoms of nations." Notice especially the use of the plural designation, kingdoms of nations. Isaiah and many of the prophets predicted the fall of Babylon to the Medes and the Persians which was accomplished when Cyrus entered the city on October 29, 539 B.C. It is startling to note that in Isaiah 45 Cyrus is named by God 150 years before his birth as the one anointed for this task. God said that He would subdue the nations before him and loose the loins of kings. In Daniel 5, where the events in Babylon the night it fell to Cyrus are described firsthand, we are told in verse 6 that the joints of King Belshazzar's loins were loosed and his knees smote one against another. The prophecy of Isaiah also states that God would "open before him the two leaved gates; and the gates shall not be shut."[20] To conquer the city, Cyrus diverted the flow of the river Euphrates so his men could enter the city of Babylon by coming in under the wall. When they came to the main bridge that spanned the river in the center of the city, they encountered brass gates which on this fateful night had not been shut. They were left open, exactly as God had promised they would be, and Cyrus was able to take the city of Babylon without destroying its mammoth walls or its magnificent buildings. Babylon continued to exist as a great and powerful city for many years. In fact, years later Alexander the Great conquered the city, taking it from the Persians and residing there until his death. Many other Bible prophecies, however, speak of the utter destruction of Babylon, predictions that as yet have not been fulfilled. For instance, Isaiah 13:5 speaks of the Lord mustering His host for battle with the weapons of His indignation from far countries from the end of heaven. This bears striking resemblance to what has happened in the gulf region during the time of the multinational conflict.

The United States, which could be described as being "from the end of heaven" from Iraq, gathered with many nations and inflicted heavy destruction upon Babylon. Isaiah 13:19 also declares that "Babylon, the glory of kingdoms, the beauty of the Chaldees' excellency, shall be as when God overthrew Sodom and Gomorrah. It shall never be inhabited, neither shall it be dwelt in from generation to generation." Chapter 14 seems to place this prophecy at the time when God will bring Israel back to its own land. Jeremiah 50 and 51 also provide interesting insights into the destruction of Babylon. Jeremiah relates God's word that He will bring against Babylon "an assembly of great nations from the north country and they shall set themselves in array against her; from thence shall she be taken; their arrows shall be as a mighty expert man; none shall return in vain."[21] We have watched with amazement the deadly accuracy of smart bombs and guided missiles as they have systematically destroyed their targets in Iraq. Jeremiah continues, "Because of the wrath of the Lord, it shall not be inhabited, but it shall be wholly desolate."[22] This total destruction is related to the time that the Israelites have again been brought back to their own land and God pardoned them. Jeremiah has declared that Babylon would become a desolation among the nations as the Lord opened His armory and brought forth His weapons of indignation against the land of the Chaldeans. God said, "Come against her from the utmost borders," that is, from the ends of the earth. "Open her storehouses, cast her up as heaps, and destroy her utterly; let nothing of her be left."[23] God promised that all of her men of war would be cut off in that day. It is interesting that the strategy used in the gulf war was to cut off the supplies to the Iraqi army stationed in Kuwait. Again in the prophecies of both Jeremiah and Isaiah, God predicts that the destruction will be as when God overthrew Sodom and Gomorrah. The prophecies tell of people coming from the north, and a great nation, and many kings being raised up from the coasts of the earth. Jeremiah 51:1 speaks of God raising up against Babylon a destroying storm. It is notable that the code name of the United Nations' operation was Desert Storm.

Babylon is known as the cradle of civilization. It is thought that the Garden of Eden was located in this area because the river Euphrates is named as one of the five rivers flowing through the Garden. If so, it is the place of the beginning of man's rebellion against God, for there Adam and Eve ate of the forbidden fruit. We also know that Babylon is the birthplace of every false religious system. Revelation 17 speaks of "Mystery Babylon the great, the mother of harlots." Harlotry, in a spiritual sense, is a reference to any false system of worship that captures the heart of man. Babylon was the mother or the birthplace of all false religions. This is where astrology was born, as man sought to understand the influence that the heavens had over destiny. Babylon was also the birthplace of commercialism. When the Jews were carried away as captives to Babylon, many of them embraced this commercial spirit and became such successful businessmen that they did not have any desire to return to Jerusalem when the opportunity arose. In Revelation 18 we read of the judgment of God that will come against the center of the commercial systems of the world, which is referred to as Babylon. It seems fitting indeed that when God begins His judgment of the world, He would begin in Babylon, the place that gave birth to so many forms of rebellion against God. But as Isaiah 13 points out, His judgment soon reaches out into the whole world to punish it for its evil.

There appear to be many parallels between what Jeremiah was saying and the events surrounding the gulf war of 1991. Babylon was to become a heap.

It was to become a dwelling place for dragons, an astonishment, and a hissing without an inhabitant. It was easy to wonder, are we on the way to seeing this prophecy fulfilled? But a significant part of the puzzle simply does not fit. The fiftieth chapter of Jeremiah tells us that this utter destruction of Babylon will come at the time when God again is dealing with the nation of Israel in grace. Nationally, Israel will acknowledge Jesus as the true Messiah and receive God's forgiveness for her sins. Clearly, based on the fact that the vast majority of Jewish people reject Christ, that time is yet future.

Isaiah 13 and 14 declare that God will muster his forces from a far country, from the end of heaven to destroy the whole land of Babylon. Isaiah places this destruction in the period of the Great Tribulation, a time coming upon the earth when God's wrath will be poured out against the ungodly, the sinner, the wicked, and the evil. The gulf war provided some startling parallels to the prophetic picture. And yet Isaiah went on to say that Babylon would never be inhabited, neither would it be dwelt in from generation to generation. The Arab would no longer pitch his tent there, nor would shepherds graze their flocks. It would become a dwelling place of wild beasts of the desert, and the habitation of every foul spirit.

Interestingly, Revelation 18:2 also speaks of the complete destruction of Babylon. John saw an angel from heaven who declared with a strong voice that "Babylon the great is fallen . . . and is become the habitation [or the dwelling place] of every foul spirit, and a cage of every unclean and hateful bird." This is very similar to the destruction described in Jeremiah. John tells us that Babylon will be destroyed in an hour, utterly burned with fire. We are told that the merchants of the world will stand looking at it, weeping and crying and wailing because they have been made rich by Babylon. By selling their merchandise to Babylon, they will have become wealthy, and then all of its beauty and all of its riches will be destroyed in an instant. We are told also that the sea merchants will stand back for fear of the torments of the destruction of the city of Babylon, and they also will be weeping because they had made so much money in bringing all of the merchandise to this commercial center. Again, these factors do not fit the current scenario. Today's Babylon could not be said to have enriched the merchants of the world. And yet this appears to be its future destiny. Zechariah 5 presents a vision in which an ephah, an ancient symbol of commerce, was carried away and placed on the plain of Shinar in modern Iraq. This prophecy clearly indicates that this area will become the sight of a pivotal economic boom as the end times draw near.

Following the successful end of the gulf war, the world has turned its attention to the rebuilding and restoration of this devastated region. It is estimated that it will take at least $200 billion to restore the industry, the bridges, the infrastructure of the cities, the buildings, and all that has been destroyed in Iraq and Kuwait. This seems an overwhelming obstacle to economic prosperity until one considers that both of these nations have the oil reserves to provide the money for complete rebuilding. Kuwait has been investing billions of dollars around the world because their oil revenue has provided more income than they could spend on their own nation. An estimated $100 billion of Kuwaiti money is invested in international holdings.

Following a recent morning worship service, a man in the import-export business remarked, "Interesting you should talk about what you did this morning. I just received a call from an official of the Kuwaiti government. He's ordered 1,000 Chevrolets from me. He said, 'Money is no object.'" A second man, who is in the oil fire control business shared that he had been offered more than $150,000 to go to Kuwait for three weeks' work. It is easy to see where the center of world commerce is shifting to these days. The gulf nations will be spending huge amounts of money to recover from this conflict. The merchants of the world are going to be made rich as they sell the steel, the technology for the refineries, the concrete, and all of the things that are necessary to put these nations back together.

It is interesting to note that Isaiah 13 ties the destruction of Babylon with the beginning of the Great Tribulation period. In the first five verses Isaiah tells of the destruction of Babylon, but he then goes on to describe events that will take place in the Great Tribulation period. Verse 6 begins with the words, "Howl, for the day of the Lord is at hand; it shall come as a destruction from the Almighty." He tells how men's hearts will melt because of the fear that grips them. When Jesus described the Great Tribulation in Luke 21, He spoke of "men's hearts failing them for fear, and for looking after those things which are coming upon the earth."[24] Again it is interesting to note that when the Scud missiles fell on Tel Aviv, there were many casualties but only three reported deaths. The deaths, however, were not attributed to the actual blast of the missiles, but rather to heart attacks as "men's hearts failed them for the fear of the things that were coming upon them."

The fact that the destruction is compared to Sodom and Gomorrah by both prophets is significant. It would seem that God is trying to give us a clue to further truth. When we look at the destruction of Sodom and Gomorrah, we remember the story of Abraham. He was sitting in the door of his tent in the heat of the day when he saw three men standing by him. He invited them to stay for a while that he might wash their feet and give them some bread. Abraham hurried to prepare a meal, and this threesome gave him the news that his wife Sarah would have a son. Sarah who was in the tent door listening to the conversation, laughed within herself at the promise. As the men rose up to continue their journey toward Sodom, one of them questioned whether they should hide from Abraham what they were going to do there. They told Abraham that because the sin of Sodom was very grievous they were going down to destroy the city. As Abraham asked if they would destroy the righteous with the wicked, he said, "Shall not the Judge of the earth do right?"[25] It was Abraham's promise that it would not be just for God to bring His wrath upon the righteous when the purpose of judgment was to deal with the wicked. Abraham questioned, "What if there are 50 righteous in the city, would you not spare the city for the 50 righteous?" The Lord responded that the city would be spared for the sake of the 50 righteous. Abraham continued to negotiate with the Lord until he was promised that if there were as few as ten righteous in the city, it would be spared.[26] What was the outcome? When the angels arrived at the city of Sodom at evening, Lot, the nephew of Abraham, was sitting in the gate of the city and insisted that they spend the night at his house. He prepared a feast for them, but before they could bed down for the night there was a commotion at the front door. The men of the city of Sodom had encircled the house and demanded that the two men be sent out to them that they might be sexually assaulted. Lot pleaded with the men of the city not to do such wickedness to his guests, and they began to turn against him, making threats upon his life. The angels pulled Lot back into the house and smote the men who were at the door with blindness. They then urged Lot to gather his family and flee from the city, for they were going to destroy it. In the morning the men hurried Lot, with his wife and two daughters, out of the city. They urged him to move quickly as they could not bring destruction until he was safely removed.

When Peter in his second epistle warns of the judgment of God that is coming upon the wicked, he points out that in the history of God's judgment, He has spared the righteous. He spared Noah by instructing him to build the ark to take him safely through the destroying flood, and He delivered righteous Lot, who was vexed by the filthy way the wicked were living. Peter comments, "For the Lord knoweth how to deliver the godly out of temptations, and to reserve the unjust unto the day of judgment to be punished."[27] So Noah can be seen as a type of the 144,000 Jews who are sealed to go through the Tribulation and Lot as a type of the Church that is removed before the judgment falls. Along with the destruction of Babylon, Isaiah 13 tells of the day of the Lord's wrath and fierce anger that will destroy sinners. He speaks of the events of the Great Tribulation period as a time when the stars of heaven do not give their light and the sun is darkened. He declares that God is going to punish the world for its evil, and the wicked for their iniquity, that mankind for the most part will be destroyed. The heavens will be shaken and the earth moved out of its place by the wrath of the Lord and His fierce anger. It is comforting to know that according to the Word of God spoken through Paul to the Thessalonians, God has not appointed us unto such wrath.[28] The Lord will surely deliver the Church before His day of judgment falls even as He delivered Lot, for the Lord of the earth is just. Paul tells us that the Lord Himself "shall descend from heaven with a shout, with the voice of the archangel, and with the trump of God; and the dead in Christ shall rise first. Then we which are alive and remain shall be caught up together with them in the clouds, to meet the Lord in the air, and so shall we ever be with the Lord." He then told us to comfort one another with these words.[29]

As we look at the world conditions today, we see what Jesus described as "the distress of nations with perplexity."[30] The word translated "perplexity" literally means "no way out." We have in the United States great economic problems. Many of the savings and loans have failed, the banking industry is tottering, people are losing their confidence in financial institutions. We see gang war on the streets of our major cities that has claimed many more lives than conflict in the Persian Gulf. We have tremendous substance-abuse problems with alcohol and other forms of drugs which are effectively destroying millions of people in our nation. We see the rapid deterioration of our public school system. The moral climate of our nation is beginning to parallel that of Sodom and Gomorrah. We have a liberal media that feeds lies to the public as it seeks to destroy anything that is righteous or godly. We have rap and rock groups that encourage children to participate in violent behavior and perverted sex acts. We have a government that spends our money to support artists who portray every kind of blasphemous attack against decency. You would think that with the huge national debt that has destroyed our economic system our government would quit financing artistic works that are no more than a thinly veiled cover for pornography.

Many sexually transmitted diseases including herpes, penicillin-resistant strains of gonorrhea and AIDS are reaching epidemic proportions. AIDS alone has caused over 100,000 deaths. We have problems with water pollution, air pollution, and mind pollution. How can we endure such dismal prospects for the future? We realize that the world copes by turning to many escape mechanisms.

Many people use alcohol as a means to escape the problems of life. Still others seek to hide from reality through both prescription and illegal drug abuse. The pleasure mania that fills our nation is a part of the attempt of man to escape thinking about the hard facts of modern living. We seek to lose ourselves in stories and dramas that remove us from real life into a fantasy world.

Some people portray pastors who speak of the coming of the Lord Jesus Christ as prophets of doom and gloom. The true doom-and-gloom prophets are the newscasters who tell us nightly what is happening in the cold, cruel world in which we live. In contrast, we as Christians have a glorious hope for the future. In spite of the hopelessness of the world and the inability of government to solve our problems, there is a new day coming. Jesus Christ promised that He would return to establish God's kingdom upon the earth. His instruction to pray that His kingdom might come and that His will would be done in earth even as it is in heaven is more relevant today than ever. The Bible, which has so accurately predicted future events, has also told us of a perfect world order that is coming. It speaks of a world where there will be no sickness, handicaps, death, sorrow, or pain; a world without pollution, crime, prisons, or war. The vast sums of money that have been spent by the nations for making destructive weapons will be diverted into agricultural development as they beat their swords into plowshares. This is far from doom and gloom. It is the only real hope for the future.

When Jesus spoke of the signs which would indicate that His return was near, He described the very events that we see happening today. He told us that when we see these things begin to come to pass we should look up and lift up our heads, for our redemption is getting close. Over and over He warned of the necessity of watching and being ready. The question each of us must ask ourselves right now is, "Am I ready to meet the Lord?" When Jesus comes to take His Church out of this world, those who do not go up in the Rapture will be left to face the terrible wrath of God that will be poured out upon the wicked and evil world. As Isaiah said, "Howl, for the day of the Lord is at hand."[31] When the day of the Lord comes each of us will be in one of two conditions: believing in Jesus or not believing in Jesus, in Christ or out of Christ, saved from the wrath to come or lost. We really have no time to waste. Each one of us needs to make our decision now.

Electronic Funds Transfer

We are told in the Scriptures that the Antichrist will cause everyone to receive a number or mark on his right hand or forehead. No one will be able to buy or sell without this number.[32] This may sound impossible, but in the seventies we began to accustom ourselves to a cashless society. Various banks offered services using little plastic cards which held coded numbers. It was possible to go to the store with a card instead of cash. The clerk processed our transaction and with a simple signature we could obtain almost any item without the exchange of money.

The day is coming when money will have absolutely no value in buying or selling. The Antichrist will base his commercial program upon a system that transfers funds with coded identification numbers. All transactions will be processed electronically by computer. Those who are on earth after the rapture of the Church will be assigned a number or mark. No one will be able to buy or sell unless they have that mark.

On the front of my new Visa card there is an account number. But that number doesn't have all the information the card contains. Much more is actually coded on a strip of magnetic tape on the back of the card. The new computer relays are able to read my credit limit and other pertinent information placed upon the tape. All major credit cards carry that magnetic tape, which has been specifically designed for the new computer relays. Both Visa and MasterCard are offering new automatic debit capabilities through the use of their cards. Through this service, a written check is unnecessary; the card transfers the funds without a paper transaction.

Soon every store will be able to set your card in a computer relay at the point of sale and automatically transfer the cost of the goods from your account to theirs. Many of the major grocery market chains already have automated teller services available.

One large market chain in southern California was losing $20,000 a month in bad checks. To solve the problem, the computer industry developed a relay tied to the banks. Now the cashiers know whether or not you have money in the bank before they accept your check. You place your supermarket card with your check in the relay and your check is either cleared or rejected. It's an excellent system and saves the markets considerable amounts of money.

Presently, most of the banks in the United States have installed computers, making it possible to offer more extensive services than ever before. Some offer a service that pays your monthly utility bills directly from your account. At the end of the month your bank statement shows how much money was taken from your account for each utility company. You never have to write a check or spend the postage to mail it. Electronic Funds Transfer (EFT) saves you all the trouble!

Currently, our whole economy seems outdated and confused. EFT is an ideal system, because it eliminates the millions of checks each bank must process annually. All transactions for goods and services are done by computers. It's an extremely efficient answer to many enormous banking problems.

EFT would also provide an ideal way of controlling theft. If no one can buy or sell without access to a computerized system, a thief wouldn't be able to sell his stolen goods without producing an identification number. But the computer would have all the information for each person using the system, and the thief would soon be apprehended. Stealing money would be useless because a person wouldn't be able to buy or sell with money. People's accounts would be safely tucked into the memory chip of a master computer that keeps track of their records. Think of all the crime this would eliminate. There would be no more liquor store holdups or service station robberies. It's a perfect solution for many of today's business and social problems.

In Europe, the World Banking Association already has an international money transfer system in operation called SWIFT (Society For Worldwide Interbank Financial Telecommunications). The Burroughs Corporation has installed two large computer operations, the main system in Brussels and a backup system in Amsterdam, Holland. The purpose of SWIFT is to make international banking transfers for all the major banks of the world. Funds can now be transferred internationally in minutes rather than the weeks it took under the old system. The computer automatically changes pounds to lira or dollars to francs, making whatever exchange is necessary.

Sixty major banks in the United States went online with SWIFT in Brussels on September 26, 1977. On October 19, 1977, the system was formally inaugurated when Prince Albert of Belgium pushed the golden button before a gathered group of dignitaries from all over the world.

In America, we are well on our way to a cashless society. Many major companies no longer issue payroll checks, but will automatically put funds in your bank account so that you don't need to handle cash. You can use credit cards to make most of your purchases.

However, there is one major problem with the credit card system. How can the retailer be certain that the person presenting the card is the one entitled to its use?

Most criminals arrested in California carry from five to 30 stolen credit cards. When a thief steals a wallet, he's usually more interested in the credit cards than the money. With a credit card he can rob an entire account or immediately charge merchandise for future resale before the card is reported stolen.

Researchers are presently working on a foolproof identification system to eliminate the problem of lost or stolen credit cards. One of the suggestions is to use a laser tattoo. A laser beam has been developed that can painlessly brand livestock in one thirty-two thousandth of a second.

Laser beams are also being used for microdata processing. Using this technology, the entire Bible can now be printed on the head of a pin. It would be very easy to write a miniaturized complete personal history so small as to be invisible, and have it placed on a convenient spot on your body (such as your hand) by laser beam. I don't know whether or not a laser tattoo will be the ultimate solution to the credit card system's identification problems, but it does present a very plausible answer. The tattooing would be totally painless and would provide a surefire form of identification that no one could duplicate or steal.

Another suggestion to solve the problem of identity is to insert a computer chip under the skin that could be read by a scanner. This is presently being done to horses to identify ownership. Also, a pilot program in Colorado Springs is inserting computer chips in dogs containing the identity and address of the owner.

The Bible states that the man who will arise from a confederation of European nations to rule the world will order everyone to receive a mark either on his right hand or on his forehead, and that no one will be able to buy or sell without this mark. It looks as if we're coming close to this today. Grocery stores already have cash registers where the checker runs a little electronic scanner over the uniform product code (UPC) on the items that you have selected. It would be very simple to hold your hand with its tattooed mark or number under the scanner so that your total grocery bill would be automatically deducted from your computerized bank account. The capacities for such procedures have already been developed and the possibilities of application are endless.

The whole world economic system is moving toward the standardized system of Electronic Funds Transfer. More and more we see the fantastic bookkeeping capacities of computers and the tremendous advantages that can be gained by using them. What the Bible predicted nearly 2,000 years ago was a scientific fantasy at the time, but it has become a practical reality today with the development of computer technology.

The Stage Is Set

According to biblical prophecy, the nation Israel had to be reborn so that the rest of the end-times prophecies could be fulfilled. Israel's national revival was a vital prop that had to be set on stage before the final act in the drama of man's history could unfold. At four in the afternoon, local time, on May 14, 1948, David Ben-Gurion proudly pulled himself up to his full height in the crowded Tel Aviv Museum and read these fateful words: "It is the self-evident right of the Jewish people to be a nation as all other nations, its own Sovereign State. Accordingly, we meet in solemn assembly today. Thus, by virtue of the natural and historic right of the Jewish people and the Resolution of the General Assembly of the United Nations, we hereby proclaim the establishment of the Jewish State in Palestine to be called the State of Israel."

Thus God has set on the stage the key players. The row of dominoes is aligned. Israel is again in her historic homeland. The ten European nations have come together and the Electronic Funds Transfer system is already in operation. There remains one event to trigger the chain reaction that will culminate in the return of Jesus Christ. The ten-nation confederacy cannot step into control until God reckons with the atheistic nation of Russia and the Church is taken out at the Rapture.

Prophetically speaking, it is not clear which imminent event, the Soviet invasion of Israel or the Rapture of the Church, will occur first. Either prediction could be fulfilled first, with the other soon following. The Church may or may not see Russia invade Israel. It's not necessary that we do. But it is certain that before the "man of sin" is revealed, the Church will be taken out.

Paul said, "Now we beseech you, brethren, by the coming of our Lord Jesus Christ, and by our gathering together unto him, that ye be not soon shaken in mind, or be troubled, neither by spirit, nor by word, nor by letter as from us, as that the day of Christ is at hand."[33]

In other words, Jesus hadn't come yet. Some people had said that He had already come and established His kingdom. "Not so!" answers Paul. "Let no man deceive you by any means, for that day shall not come, except there come a falling away first."[34]

The term "falling away" is an interesting translation of the Greek word *apostasia*. The root verb from which apostasia comes means "to depart from." This verb is used 15 times in the New Testament and only once translated "fall away." In other instances it is translated "to depart from" or "to leave from."

William Tyndale, one of the first people to translate the Bible into English, and many other early translators of the New Testament, rendered apostasia as "a departure." If this is the case, this verse can be read, "For the day shall not come, except there come a departure first, and that man of sin be revealed, the son of perdition." This "falling away" could very easily refer to the departure, or rapture, of the Church.

Paul continues, "The mystery of iniquity doth already work: only he who now letteth [is hindering] will let [will hinder], until he be taken out of the way. And then shall that Wicked [one] be revealed, whom the Lord shall . . . destroy with the brightness of his coming. Even him, whose coming is after the working of Satan with all power and signs and lying wonders, and with all deceivableness of unrighteousness in them that perish; because they received not the love of the truth, that they might be saved."[35]

The Antichrist will be revealed to those who shall perish, because they did not receive the love of the truth that they might be saved. He cannot be revealed until he who hinders is taken out of the way. The hindering force that is keeping the Antichrist from being revealed today is the power of the Holy Spirit working within the Church. Notice the Antichrist will come to those who are unrighteous, those who are to perish because they would not receive the truth. Nowhere in the Scriptures is there any mention of the Church being on the earth during the reign of the Antichrist. We are told that Antichrist makes war with the saints and overcomes them in Revelation 13:7. But those saints cannot be the Church as is manifestly evident by the statement of Jesus in Matthew 16:18: "I will build my church, and the gates of hell shall not prevail against it." It is clear then that only after Jesus Christ takes His Church away will the man of sin be revealed. The Antichrist will then be free to establish a covenant with Israel and promise to help them rebuild their temple.

When I have talked with Israelis over the past several years, they have tried to explain to me why they do not believe that Jesus is the Messiah. It seems that the claim that He is the Son of God is a stumbling block to them. Yet they are hard-pressed to explain Isaiah 9:6, where the prophet through the Spirit said, "For unto us a child is born, unto us a son is given; and the government shall be upon his shoulder, and his name shall be called Wonderful, Counselor, the Mighty God, the Everlasting Father, the Prince of Peace." I've often asked them the simple question, "Who gave His Son?"

Many Jews feel that the Messiah will be a man just as Moses was. They quote the words of Moses himself found in Deuteronomy 18:15: "The Lord thy God will raise up into thee a Prophet from the midst of thee, of thy brethren, like unto me; unto him ye shall hearken." I have asked them, "If he is just a man, how will you recognize that he is the Messiah?" They responded, "Simple, He will lead us to rebuild our temple." Many of the rabbis are expecting the Messiah to come soon. In light of the fact that Daniel speaks of the covenant that the Antichrist will make with Israel and the prophecy of Jesus in John 5:43, when He told the Jews, "I am come in my Father's name, and ye receive me not. If another shall come in his own name, him ye will receive," it is easy to see just how ready so many are to accept the false Messiah.

The Antichrist will make a covenant with Israel which will no doubt include the authorization to rebuild the temple on its historic sight. But Daniel tells us that he will break the covenant and set up the abomination which will cause the desolation, or the Great Tribulation. This abomination will consist of the Antichrist standing in the temple of God claiming to be God, and demanding to be worshiped as God.

It is interesting to see the great desire by many Jews in Israel to rebuild the temple today. Dr. Assur Koffman, a professor at the Hebrew University in Jerusalem, is a part of this movement. He has been engaged in extensive research to locate the possible site of Solomon's Temple, and has concluded that it stood some 322 feet north of the Dome of the Rock. According to his investigation, the Holy of Holies stood over what is known today as the Dome of the Spirits or the Dome of the Tablets. If his conclusions are correct, they would be very significant. The rebuilding of the Jewish temple could be accomplished without removing the Dome of the Rock. This would prevent a full scale Jihad (holy war) by the Muslims. This location for the temple would also have interesting ramifications in Old Testament interpretation. When Ezekiel had his vision in which he saw the rebuilt temple, he was ordered to measure it. In chapter 42:20, he tells us the temple had a wall around it about 500 feet long to make a separation between the sanctuary and the profane place.

The Dome of the Rock has approximately 700 feet of Arabic writing around the top of it, both inside and out, which seeks to profane Jesus Christ. It declares, "God is not begotten neither does He beget" which is a direct attack against the New Testament truth that "God so loved the world he gave his only begotten Son."[36]

In Revelation 11 John also had a vision of the new temple that would stand in Jerusalem during the Tribulation period. He too was ordered to measure it, but was told not to measure the outer court, as it had been given to the heathen. If the new temple were to be built with the Dome of the Spirits as the site for the Holy of Holies, the Dome of the Rock could stand behind a wall similar to the one Ezekiel measured. It would be located in the area which would have been the outer court of Solomon's Temple. I believe that building a wall just north of the Dome of the Rock, giving the Jews the north side of the Temple Mount as the site for their new temple, will be the solution offered by the Antichrist. This ingenious answer to one of the most difficult political problems ever faced by mankind will cause the Antichrist to be acclaimed by the world as a brilliant peacemaker. The Jews will hail him as the Messiah, leading to the beginning of the final seven-year week described in Daniel's prophecy.

Three and a half years later, he will return to stand in the Holy Place, and boast that he is God.[37] The Jews will then realize their mistake and flee to the wilderness where God has prepared a place to shelter them for the final 3½ years of the Antichrist's tenure. During this same period, the world will be going through a time of trouble unparalleled in its history. As Jesus said in Matthew 24:21, the tribulation will be worse than anything the world has ever seen before or will ever see again. These terrifying events are chronicled in detail in Revelation, chapters 6 through 19.

Preparation

Peter said, "Seeing then that all these things shall be dissolved, what manner of persons ought ye to be?"[38] The message of Scripture is clear. We're coming down to the final curtain. But this raises a crucial question. What kind of a people ought we to be? First of all, we should be spiritual people. God is going to shake this earth until everything that can be shaken is shaken—until only that which cannot be moved out of place will remain.[39] If our lives are invested in the spiritual, we won't lose a thing. This being so, we should be more concerned with spiritual issues than material things, with spiritual investments rather than material pursuits.

We should also be diligent. The Lord told us to "occupy" until He comes.[40] We must make it our aim to live fully each day to please Him. As we look at the world today, it would appear that the coming of the Lord is close at hand. Yet we do not know when it will be. It could be that the Lord will wait a little while longer; therefore, we must occupy till He comes.

We should live as though the Lord were coming today, because He just might. Be diligent about the things of the Lord and yet practical about your life. Don't quit your job. Don't quit school. But all the while look up and lift up your head, for your redemption is drawing nigh!

2

End Times

As we have seen, many of the main props are now in place on the world stage. The actors are taking their places and the final scene is ready to begin. The angel of the Lord told Daniel that 70 sevens are determined upon the nation Israel. Sixty-nine of those sevens have already been fulfilled.

The angel also said that the time span from the commandment to restore and rebuild Jerusalem to the coming of the Messiah would be exactly 483 years, but the Messiah would be cut off and receive nothing, and the Jews would be dispersed.[1] Just as the angel told Daniel, Jesus the Messiah was cut off without receiving His kingdom, and the Jews were dispersed by the Romans in 70 A.D.

Since the crucifixion, God's prophetic calendar has stood still. One important seven-year period, the seventieth seven of Daniel, is yet to come. This will complete the entire prophecy of Daniel 9.

In His first coming, Jesus Christ accomplished reconciliation with God by dying for our sins. He made an end of our iniquities through His death on the cross. The latter portion of that prophecy, which includes bringing in everlasting righteousness and His eternal kingdom, the completion of all prophecies, and the anointing of the most Holy, remains yet to be fulfilled. These prophetic elements will come to pass at Christ's second coming. During this last seven-year period, the man of sin, or the Antichrist, will be revealed. Jesus Christ referred to him as "the one who shall come in his own name" and whom the Jews will receive.[2] This man of sin will arise from a confederation of ten European nations. The Antichrist, as we saw earlier, will establish a completely new economic system. Financial transactions will be accomplished completely through Electronic Funds Transfer. Everyone will be assigned a mark or number. No one will be able to buy or sell without this mark. This system was prophesied in Revelation 13 almost 2,000 years ago, and today we see the development of technology that will make it a reality.

According to our government, every person in the United States will soon be assigned a new identification number.[3] Social Security cards are simply too easy to obtain; in fact, many people already have several. Because of the great number of illegal aliens that have flooded into the United States, the government has declared this new identification system necessary. The new identification number will be given to each citizen for life. The government plans to assign this number to each baby the moment it is born. This system will eliminate the present confusion in identification. However, as long as the number is on a card, whether paper or plastic, the possibility of forgery, theft, or simply borrowing someone else's number exists.

As a woman in the grocery store pulled her credit card out of her purse, she said, "Wouldn't it be nice if they could attach this thing to my body so I wouldn't lose it anymore?" This woman was on to something. "They" won't affix a credit card to your body, but there will be another classification system worked out. No man will be able to buy or sell unless he has his identification mark in his right hand or his forehead.

Today, this checkless cashless economic system is technically possible. As we have already seen, international banks are using Electronic Funds Transfers. In fact, the amount of money presently transferred through the EFT System in the United States every week is greater than the amount of our national debt. As these developments progress, it seems inevitable that the new economy predicted in the Bible is on its way!

Russian Power

The Bible predicts a ten-nation European confederacy will rise to power and become the last world-governing empire. But as we noted earlier, the Soviet Union presents a major stumbling block to the EEC's becoming a world-governing power. The EEC cannot rise to predicted prominence as long as the USSR poses such a tremendous threat to the European continent.

Many of our military strategists believe that the Soviet Union, without the use of nuclear weapons, but just by the vast superiority of personnel and conventional weaponry, could conquer all of Western Europe in seven days. The situation is well in hand though, as God has a unique plan to take care of the Soviet Union.

How will God remove the USSR as a major military threat? How will ten European nations become a world power? And how will the Antichrist take over as the leader of these ten nations and bring the world under his power? The answers are found in the prophecies of Ezekiel.

In chapter 37, Ezekiel has a vision of a valley of dry bones. God asked the prophet, "Can these bones be made to live again?" Ezekiel said, "Lord, you know." Then he watched the valley as the dry bones came together—and formed a skeleton. Then Ezekiel saw flesh form upon the skeleton; muscles developed, and it stood upright. God prophesied to Ezekiel, "So I will make my people to live again, though they have been scattered. I will bring them back into the land, and they shall dwell there. I will put my Spirit in them, and I will plant them in the land. I will put flesh upon them, and I will put muscle upon them." God was speaking of how He would gloriously resurrect the nation of Israel in the last days.[4] Then in chapter 38, God said, "When I have brought them back into the land, I will put an evil thought into the minds of the leaders of Magog."[5] Magog, throughout history, has been known as that vast area north of the Caucasus Mountains. Today it is known as the USSR. God continued, "I will bring thee [Russia] out of the north quarters and all of thy bands with thee."[6]

God even listed the nations that would be allied with the Soviet Union. In most cases, the countries God listed are within the Soviet sphere of influence today. But there will be a few changes. For instance, Iran will ultimately side with Russia against Israel, an alliance that is presently being formed. God then said, "I will bring thee forth with all your bands against the nation of Israel. I will put hooks into your jaw and I will lead thee forth."[7] God is going to lead the Soviet Union into Israel for the slaughter. He declared, "When you have come in to the mountains of Israel, my fury shall arise in my face and I will turn thee back."[8] God then describes the destruction that will fall upon this invading Russian army.

In chapter 39, God gives us the details of the overwhelming defeat. He will leave but a sixth of the invading Russian army: Five-sixths will be destroyed! The Israelis will spend seven years burning the implements of war. Seven months after the battle is over, professional men will begin burying the bones of the dead soldiers.

It is a fascinating point that Israel will not start burying the dead for seven months. It is also interesting to note that nobody will touch those bones but will wait for men hired specifically for the purpose of burying them to do the job. When a person sees a skeleton, he will place a marker by it so this troop of grave diggers can come and dispose of the carcasses that have fallen in the land of Israel. Remember this fact. Later on we'll examine the significance of this prophecy in light of the present nuclear potential of the Israelis.

God declared, "When I have brought them again from the people, and gathered them out of their enemies' lands, and am sanctified in them in the sight of many nations, then shall they know that I am the Lord their God. . . . Neither will I hide my face any more from them." Notice the three important declarations here. At this time the Jews (Israel) would know that the Lord is God, God's face would no longer be hidden from them, and the Holy Spirit would be poured out on the house of Israel.[9]

This is a significant moment. We are told that God will again pour out His Spirit on the nation of Israel in the day He destroys the Russian army. Earlier in his prophecy, Ezekiel saw the glory of God depart from the temple in Jerusalem.[10] Jesus prophesied in Matthew 23:38 that their house would be left desolate or deprived of God's presence. When God again pours out His Spirit upon the nation Israel, His great time clock will be started once again. The world will be at the beginning of the last seven-year period.

The Soviet invasion of Israel plays a key part in the total plan of God. This military invasion will actually trigger the beginning of the end. Once the last seven-year period is finished, Jesus Christ will come again in glory and will be anointed as King of Kings and Lord of Lords. Then God's everlasting kingdom will be established upon the earth.

It is my very strong conviction that before God's Spirit is placed upon Israel, the Church will be taken out of the earth. The Bible says, "Blindness in part is happened to Israel, until the fullness of the Gentiles be come in."[11] When God no longer blinds the nation of Israel, but has poured His Spirit upon His people, the Church will be precluded from being here. Today the Spirit of God has been moving upon the Gentile world, drawing out a bride for Jesus Christ. But when that body of believers is completed, when the fullness of Gentiles has come in, then God's Spirit will deal with the nation Israel. God will take them back and acknowledge them as His people once again. The decisive defeat of the Russian army will give the European nations the opportunity to rise to immediate power. This confederacy will then be the unchallenged major power on the European continent. The Russian invasion of Israel appears to be the next major event on the prophetic horizon.

Close Call

I would like to point out how close we came to the end of the Church age in October 1973. During Yom Kippur (the holiest day of the year for the Jews), Syria and Egypt simultaneously attacked Israel from opposite ends of the country. The majority of the Israelis including the regular army personnel were in their synagogues or resting quietly at home. Communication networks had been silent all day in respect of the holy day. Suddenly, sirens began to wail in Tel Aviv and Jerusalem. Radios immediately came alive with emergency code numbers for the nation's military troops.

The call also went out to the people in the reserve to activate and defend themselves. The Syrians and Egyptians had launched what was intended to be the "war of annihilation." The Syrians attacked the Golan Heights with 1,200 tanks in an initial assault over a 20-mile area. (When Hitler made his major invasion of the Soviet Union in World War II, he used 1,000 tanks over a 200-mile perimeter.) In the Sinai, Egypt attacked with 3,000 tanks and 1,000 pieces of major artillery. It was intended to be the complete destruction of the nation of Israel, and the Arab powers almost achieved their goal. Were it not for miracles which were greater than those that took place during the 1967 war, Israel would not be a nation today. Miracles as great as those in Bible days took place when this Arab confederacy attacked Israel with vast superiority in numbers and weaponry.

From this near disaster rose many stories of bravery and personal heroism. As Zechariah prophesied, some of the insignificant soldiers became as David.[12] Consider the case of Lieutenant Zvi Greengold, a man who would come to be known by the nickname "Zwicka." Lieutenant Greengold was with his family at Kibbutz Lochamei Hagetaot when the war broke out. He immediately put on his uniform and hitchhiked to the headquarters at Nafech on the Golan front. He asked for a tank command and was told that two damaged tanks were coming in for repairs. With only one other operational tank available, he would head the Zwicka Unit on the Tapline route.

Lieutenant Greengold soon found himself in the thick of battle. He managed to knock out several Syrian tanks but in the meantime saw his own support tanks go down. He realized that he would have to leave the main road to survive, and began maneuvering from behind the knolls that parallel the highway. Zwicka would come up over a small hill, destroy one of the Syrian tanks, then race behind the hilly ground and repeat his action. He was knocking out so many tanks that the Syrians thought a whole Israeli tank brigade was facing them. Believing themselves to be outmanned, they retreated!

With odds of 50 to 1 against him, Zwicka turned back the Syrian attack that day. He kept radioing the headquarters that the Zwicka unit had destroyed another Syrian tank, leading headquarters to think that Zwicka was a whole armored unit. But this brave soldier was out there all alone, holding off the Syrian advance. His is only one of countless stories of David-like heroism to come out of the Yom Kippur War.

The Syrians easily poured through the southern section of the Golan Heights where Israeli defenses had been depleted. They came within one mile of the Golani headquarters of the Israeli Army. At the time the Syrians approached this base of operations, the Israelis had only two tanks and ten men to defend the headquarters. It seems strange that wave after wave of Syrian tanks moved in, but stopped a mile from this strategic outpost. Later the Golan Heights commander laughed and said the Syrians had an excellent view of the Sea of Galilee and stopped to admire it. He confesses that he really doesn't know why they stopped their unrestrained advance.

It is speculated that since the Syrians weren't able to move through the northern sector, they may have suspected that the Israelis were letting them pour freely through on the south in order to trap them. The Syrians didn't know that on the first day of the war they could have moved all the way to Tiberias. They could have taken the whole Galilee region.

Down in the Sinai, the Egyptians were planning to take the Bar-Lev line within 24 hours. They took it in just five hours. They were so surprised with their quick success that they decided to wait there. They didn't have any contingency plans for moving further so soon. They were not aware that the only obstacles between them and Tel Aviv were 90 battered Israeli tanks. Mysteriously, both the Syrians and the Egyptians halted long enough to give the Israelis a chance to mobilize their reserve units and counterattack both in the Golan Heights and in the Sinai.

When the Israelis began their assault in the Golan Heights, they pushed the Syrians back until Israeli tank units came within 12 miles of Damascus. Israel then brought in its artillery units to bombard the Syrian capital. In a brilliant move in the Sinai, General Ariel Sharon crossed the Suez Canal with an assault force and trapped the entire Egyptian Third Army on the Sinai Peninsula. The Egyptians were totally dependent upon the Israelis for their food and medicine.

Just hours after the war had started, Soviet Premier Brezhnev cabled President Nixon and told him that the Soviet Union would begin unilateral action to bring an enforced "peace" to the Middle East. Ironically, Soviet cargo planes were on their way to the region before the war ever started. As early as October 6, 1973, Russian ships landed in Alexandria, Egypt, and in the Syrian port of Latakia with war supplies.

Three days before hostilities began the USSR sent up spy satellites designed to photograph and monitor Israel. The Arab attack was originally scheduled for 6:00 P.M. on Yom Kippur, but satellite data showed the Israelis had begun to mobilize, so the attack was moved ahead by four hours. Soviet soldiers were manning some of the invading tanks because Syria didn't have enough trained personnel to do the job. Many Soviet soldiers driving Syrian tanks were captured by the Israelis on the Golan Heights, a fact which was later hushed up.

We were in Israel during the Yom Kippur War. On our way from Tel Aviv to our hotel in Bat Yom, we were talking to our cab driver. He was a lieutenant in the army and we were his last fare before he had to report for duty. We told him we'd be praying for him because this time it looked as if the war was really a tough one.

He said, "Yes, it is. We're fighting the Russians this time."

I agreed and said, "The Russians have moved in some advanced equipment. The SAM-6's are really potent missiles. You're fighting against sophisticated Russian weapons this time."

He said, "I didn't say Russian weapons. We're fighting against the Russians. We've already captured several of them in the Golan Heights."

The capture of Russian personnel in the Golan Heights was reported in *Time* magazine, then mysteriously hushed.

In a single air battle in the Sinai, five Russian MIGs were shot down. All five were piloted by Red Army personnel. The Soviets had moved a heavy cruiser with nuclear warheads on its decks into Alexandria. This was spotted by U.S. reconnaissance.

When Brezhnev notified President Nixon that the USSR would take unilateral action to bring peace to the Middle East, he was saying that they were preparing to invade Israel. The war had started to turn against Egypt and Syria. In fact, the Russian cargo planes that were bringing supplies were reassigned and were being loaded with Soviet paratroopers. The Red Army was planning to launch a paratroop attack against Israel.

When the Soviets took over Czechoslovakia during the rebellion in 1968, the first thing they did was to send in paratroopers to take over the airport. Once Red Army troops captured the airport and sealed it off, they immediately brought in their supplies and tanks and were able to move from the heart of the country to put down the rebellion. It's a typical Soviet tactic of warfare.

Therefore, when Brezhnev cabled the threat to Nixon, our president put U.S. troops on alert around the world. Kissinger began fast-paced trips from Israel to Syria to Cairo in an effort to hammer out a peace settlement and a quick cease-fire before the Russians moved in. For a moment, World War III was in the offing. We came close to seeing the end in 1973, but God had other purposes. He brought the war to a halt.

Looking back, the Israelis feel that they made a mistake in halting their advance. They were robbed of a full and decisive victory over the Arabs. They could have fired on Damascus with their tanks, forcing the city to surrender. General Sharon was pleading for permission to move against Cairo while he had the momentum going for him, and the Egyptian army trapped and helpless. But he was stopped by U.S. pressure, and the Jews were kept from a total victory. As a result, the Israelis feel today that they're right back where they started.

Syria has now doubled its arsenal of weapons compared to the beginning of the Yom Kippur War. Some sources say that it has even tripled its strength. Over 1,200 Russian advisers have instructed the Iraqis in the use of thousands of tanks, planes and the now famous Scud Missile which the Soviets supplied. As the gulf war revealed, Israel is now easily within range of a number of hostile Arab powers. The USSR is giving tremendous military support to Syria, Iraq, and the Arab states.

Again in 1982 it was apparent that the Soviet Union was planning to aid an attack on Israel. Many Israeli military officers believe that the move by the Israeli army into southern Lebanon in June thwarted a planned fall invasion. As the Israeli army moved north in their Peace for Galilee operation, they were amazed at the vastness of the store of weapons they discovered. Prime Minister Menachem Begin declared that even though Israeli Intelligence is one of the best in the world and knew that weapons were being stored in southern Lebanon, the amount of weapons captured was 10 times greater than had been expected. It took over three months to transfer these weapons back to Israel, using more than a score of huge truck-and-trailer rigs operating 24 hours a day. Israel captured 400 new T-62 tanks, the plans for the proposed invasion, and enough weapons to equip three army divisions. The only place to find enough trained personnel to use such a large store of weapons would have been the Soviet Union. Again it would appear that God had allowed us a little more time before the end.

I recently saw a cartoon which depicted a little gray-bearded, robed man carrying an "end of the world is near" sign past the Pentagon as two high-ranking generals were emerging. One general turned to the other and remarked, "I thought that was classified information." We know though, that the end is near and we see it coming even closer as we watch the situation in the Middle East.

Israeli Attitude Changing

It is very interesting to notice the Israelis' change of attitude since the 1973 war. The Israelis used to have what was called "the Masada complex," the belief that suicide is preferable to slavery.

When the Roman general Silvanus was making his final assault against the elevated city of Masada in 72 A.D., the 960 inhabitants saw that a tremendous ramp had been built toward the rear of their fortress. They knew that in the morning the Romans would attack and they would not be able to hold off the assault. Ben Eleazar called the people together in the synagogue and announced that they would either see their wives ravished before their eyes, or they could take the honorable way and commit mass suicide. The people decided on suicide rather than slavery.

Each man gathered together with his family. Ten men were chosen to go through the city of Masada and systematically kill the children first, then the wife, and then the husband of each family. The husband and wife kissed their children good-bye, and the husband kissed his wife. Then they laid down on the floor and their throats were slit. The ten remaining men gathered in a room. They drew coins numbered one through ten to choose who would be the last to die. As nine men lay on the floor, the man chosen to die last slit their throats. After he made sure they were dead, he then committed suicide.

The next morning the Romans broke into the city of Masada. To their horror they discovered that the city's inhabitants were all dead, with the exception of one old lady and a few children who had hidden in a cave. It was an empty victory for Rome.

Until just recently, Jewish cadets were taken to Masada for their graduation exercises. The leaders would recount the story of Masada and then the whole group declared together, "Masada shall not fall again." In other words, they too feel that suicide is preferable to slavery. They'll fight until they die.

However, the Masada complex is being replaced in Israel by a new attitude called, "the Samson complex." Samson also committed suicide, but when he did, he took his enemies with him. When he knew it was the end, Samson had a little boy lead him to the pillars that were the main supports of the temple of his Philistine captors. When he reached the pillars, Samson bowed with all his strength and pulled the pillars in so that 3,000 Philistines were crushed along with him.[13] Today some Israeli leaders say that if they have to go, they'll take the world with them. They feel, and with good reason, that the world has let them down.

In the Yom Kippur War, after ten days of fighting, the Israelis almost ran out of ammunition. The United States could not help them because Germany, England, Italy, and France would not let U.S. supply planes land and refuel on their soil. Finally after ten days Portugal opened up a base on the Azores for refueling. U.S. planes were soon landing almost nose-to-tail at the Tel Aviv airport, resupplying the Israeli army just in time to keep them ahead in the war.

Israel feels that Europe has deserted her. She says, "If we fall, why should we care if the world also falls?"

General Ariel Sharon, who led the brilliant counterattack across the Suez Canal, said to a U.S. senator visiting Israel that if another war erupts in the Middle East, the United States won't have to worry about an Arab oil embargo. He pointed out that Entebbe (where the Israelis completed a successful commando attack) is 2,000 miles from Tel Aviv . . . but Riyadh is only 900 miles away. General Sharon said that his men would "take care" of the oil situation if there was another war.

The Israelis are planning to go all out in the next war. They have declared that they will not stop until every arm lifted against them has been destroyed. They intend to take over or destroy the Saudi Arabian oil fields. Saudi Arabia has been allocating $1 billion annually to the Arab states for the next conflict. The Israelis feel Saudi Arabia should not go unpunished. It is the Israelis' full intention that the next war will remove any chance for enemy advances. Their sole goal is a decisive victory.

What will such a decisive commitment bring? When Israel begins to exercise the advantage in the next conflict you can be sure that the Soviets will try to stop them by force. As soon as the USSR moves against Israel, the final countdown will begin. We will then be at the scene that God described in Ezekiel 38 and 39. Russia's invasion of Israel is the first event that will trigger a sequence of events during the final seven years: the emergence of the ten-nation European power, the rise of the Antichrist, the Great Tribulation during the last half of the seven years, and then the coming of Jesus Christ with His Church in power and glory! Finally, the world will see the establishment of God's kingdom bringing in everlasting righteousness.

Where does this place the Church? When God's Spirit is again poured out upon the nation of Israel and the Soviets are decisively defeated, the door will be open for the emergence of the Antichrist. We have already seen how the Antichrist cannot arise until the Church has been taken out of the way. We will literally be out of this world.

Paul said, "Behold, I show you a mystery. We shall not all sleep, but we shall all be changed, in a moment, in the twinkling of an eye."[14] We do not know exactly when the Church will be taken away in relation to the Soviet attack on Israel. The Church could be out before the Red Army ever invades Israel or during the time of the battle. We shall certainly be taken out by the time God destroys the Soviet invasion force and again puts His Spirit on the nation Israel.

War clouds are still hanging over the Middle East right now. Syria has fully armed itself and its president is threatening to forcibly recapture the Golan Heights and the West Bank. Israel refuses to give back even an inch of the occupied territories. The whole Middle East situation could explode again at any moment. Most of the Israelis with whom I've talked are anticipating conflict at any time.

If war breaks out, and it's certainly within the realm of probability, very soon we could be rejoicing around the throne of God in glory! Keep your eye on the Middle East. Things are getting more momentous there every day.

Israel's Nuclear Potential

The Israelis have indicated that they now possess nuclear weapons. In fact, during the very crucial moments early in the 1973 war, when it looked as if Israel would be defeated, it quite possibly could have been activating some of its nuclear bombs. Israel has often declared that its greatest advantage is that it can't afford to lose. In 1977 there were indications that Israel possessed a neutron bomb, a weapon the United States was still developing. The neutron bomb is that great "humanitarian weapon" that destroys people but doesn't destroy buildings or industries. It is designed to kill by ultrahigh radiation.

In his book *Hirshima* John Hersey describes the effects of the atomic bomb dropped on Hiroshima. Many people who were not killed by the initial blast died from the effects of radiation. He describes how eyeballs melted and poured down peoples' faces. Sores that would not heal broke out upon their bodies, and their flesh dissolved as a result of exposure to high radiation.[15] The effects of radiation on people from the bomb explosion in Hiroshima are identical to those the neutron bomb is designed to cause. The prospect of the use of this weapon is horrifying.

In this light Ezekiel 39 becomes intensely interesting. God specifically points out the fact that people won't touch the bones of the victims for seven months. Finally, professional buriers will be hired to bury the carcasses. Could the refusal to touch these remains be caused by fear of radioactive contamination? Ezekiel perfectly describes the results of death by radiation poisoning.

The Lord told Zechariah that His people would come back into the land of Israel, and Jerusalem would be inhabited again. Jerusalem would become "a burdensome stone" to all of her neighbors round about. Whoever sought to come against Jerusalem would be destroyed. Though the whole world gathered against her (which seems to be happening today) the Lord would defend the inhabitants of Jerusalem and the least of them "would be as David."[16]

Then the Lord said, "This shall be the plague wherewith the Lord will smite all the people that have fought against Jerusalem: Their flesh shall consume away while they stand upon their feet, and their eyes shall consume away in their holes, and their tongue shall consume away in their mouth."[17] Twenty-five hundred years ago, God described a plague remarkably similar to the effects of the intense radiation of a neutron bomb. I can't say that's exactly how Israel will defeat the Soviet Union, but certainly the description in Zechariah raises some interesting possibilities.

We are living in the last days. At any moment the Middle East could erupt into a conflict that will escalate into the "war of annihilation." Israel will be going all out, which will undoubtedly prompt Soviet involvement. Then the Lord will take us, the Body of Christ, out of the whole mad scene and into the heavenly glories of the Father where we will be sheltered until the wrath of God has been expended on the earth.

Jesus said, "When these things begin to come to pass, then look up, and lift up your heads for your redemption draweth nigh."[18]

It's later than you think! Now is the time to wake up from your lethargy and realize that the coming of the Lord is at hand. If you've been playing around with Christianity and your relationship with God, it's high time to realize you need a full-on commitment to Jesus Christ. There's no time to waste. The Bridegroom is coming. He's literally at the door, waiting to make His dramatic entrance onto the main scene. Now is the time to make sure you'll be ready when He comes.

If you wait until you read the headline "Russia Invades Israel," you may have waited too long, because the Church may not even be here to see the invasion. I would encourage you now, while you yet can, to ask God for the free gift of forgiveness and eternal life He offers you in Christ. Submit yourself to Him, and you too will rejoice at the appearing of our great God and Savior, Jesus Christ.

3

Crisis Years

World Crisis

A new and very significant development is taking place in the Middle East. The Soviet Union has sought to position itself as one of the major powers in the bringing about of a peaceful solution to the Iraqi crisis. The Soviets tried to persuade Iraq to remove her forces from Kuwait and launched a peace initiative. Saddam Hussien constantly sought to link Iraq's withdrawal from Kuwait with the withdrawal of Israel from the West Bank and the creation of a Palestinian state. The United States insisted that Iraq's withdrawal be unconditional. The U.N. coalition indicated that once the issue of Kuwait had been settled, they would take up the matter of the Palestinians. Could it be that one of the under-the-table understandings that the USSR made with Iraq is that the Soviets would push the Palestinian issue in the United Nations? If the United Nations would mandate a Palestinian state within the borders of Israel, Israel would surely fail to comply. This refusal would provide the Soviets with the excuse to create a coalition of nations to force Israel to comply with the U.N. mandate, much as the United States gathered a coalition of nations to enforce the U.N. resolutions calling for Iraq to pull out of Kuwait. The prophet Ezekiel tells us in chapter 38 that Magog, or the Soviet Union, will come with a confederation of nations against Israel in the last days. The United States could not object too strenuously, inasmuch as we have just done the same thing against Iraq. It is interesting to look at the alignment of nations that Ezekiel prophesies will be coming with the Soviets. Iran, Ethiopia, Libya, Gomer (Eastern Europe), and Togarmah (Turkey) are all specifically mentioned. It is no doubt significant that Iraq is not listed as one of the aggressive powers aligned with this coalition. Syria, Jordan, and Egypt are also conspicuous by their absence. It is also very interesting that Saudi Arabia is among the nations that will object to this move by the Soviet-led power block. Perhaps the Saudis will realize that the purpose of the USSR's desire to become a major force in the Middle East is more than just helping the unfortunate Palestinians. The motives could be much more aligned with self-interest. According to some estimates, if the USSR continues to produce oil from its reserves at the present rate, it will face total depletion by the year 2003. The desire to gain a strong foothold in the oil-rich gulf states will no doubt be the underlying motive for Soviets moving their troops into the area. This desire will not be lost on nations such as Saudi Arabia. Twice in Ezekiel 38, as the prophet speaks of this invasion, he declares that the invaders are coming to take spoil. For any nation to be a strong industrial power, oil is essential. Whether we want to admit it or not, oil is one of the major reasons that our troops were sent into the gulf, for it is necessary to protect the oil supplies that keep our nation functioning. It is estimated that at current rate of consumption our reserves of oil will run out in 2002. It would appear by the state of current events in the world that not only is oil running out, but time is running out as well. As Paul said to the Romans, "Knowing the time, that now it is high time to awake out of sleep, for now is our salvation nearer than we believed. The night is far spent, the day is at hand." It seems very significant that Isaiah 13:6 indicates that at the time Babylon is destroyed the people will howl for the day of the Lord is at hand; that is, the day when His judgment and wrath are to be poured out upon the earth. Isaiah does not declare that the day of the Lord has already begun, but the destruction of Babylon signals that the time is *at hand*. It is important to note that the outcome of this alleged peacekeeping mission by the Soviet-led coalition of nations will be far different than that in the Iraq/Kuwait conflict. In the case of Israel, the invading forces are to be destroyed by the direct intervention of God. God said that at that time, His fury would rise and that there would be a great shaking in the land of Israel, that the mountains would be thrown down, and that God would call for every man's sword to be against his own brother. This may indicate that the domestic turmoil currently brewing within the Soviet Union will come to a head and that a civil war will fragment the Red Army. Along with this infighting God will send an overflowing rain, accompanied with great hailstones, fire, and brimstone, which will spell disaster for this invasion force. The Word of God declares that from that day forward, the house of Israel will know that Yahweh is their God. With the breakup of the Warsaw Pact and the strong economic and civil problems within the Soviet Union, some have questioned the idea that the Red Army is strong enough to project its power into the Middle East. However, other experts such as retired Marine four-star general Lewis Walt strongly disagree. In his book *The Eleventh Hour*, General Walt quotes Alexander Solzhenitsyn as saying that the momentum toward war with the Soviet Union is so great that he wouldn't be surprised to see the West fall on any given morning.[1]

General Walt writes in his preface, "I have never asked Marines to go into battle without telling them exactly what they faced so far as I knew it. My one unbreakable rule has always been to stick with facts and tell the truth. That is what I'm going to do in this book. The facts are these: The United States has been brought, by its own civilian leaders, to a position of military inferiority to the Soviet Union. At this moment, you and your loved ones stand exposed to physical destruction. The option of whether you shall live or die rests primarily with the hardened men who occupy the Kremlin. If they should choose tomorrow or next year to annihilate you and your family, there is little the U.S. government could do to stop them except to surrender. No generation of Americans has ever before been so recklessly placed at the mercy of so pitiless and powerful an enemy."

In an interview with a national publication, General Rogers, former Supreme Allied Commander in Europe, was asked, "In what part of the world are we in the most danger from Soviet Russia?" As far as I know, General Rogers isn't a Bible student. Nothing in the article indicates that he is. He's purely a military strategist with the advantage of the knowledge that military intelligence has been able to gather. General Rogers answered, "I don't believe that there's going to be an attack on Western Europe by the Warsaw Pact as the beginning of a global confrontation. I think that the confrontation would erupt someplace else and spill over into Western Europe. It would probably be related to political instability in some region or the competition for scarce resources, or both. I'd say that this is most likely to occur in the Middle East–Persian Gulf–Indian Ocean area." I think his evaluation is correct from a biblical standpoint. We need to keep our eyes on the Middle East.[2]

How interesting that those of us who study biblical prophecy are no longer classified with the religious fanatics when we start talking about critical years and the end of the world. Serious-minded people looking at our world in crisis are beginning to tell us that something must be done. The usual solution provided by these men is simple and direct. We can no longer continue as separate nations with separate goals and ideals. We must surrender to a globally federated body, a one-world government. We also need a one-world religion. I recently saw a bumper sticker that read, "God is too big for one religion." Many people are dedicated to working toward these universalistic goals, which again, is exactly what the Bible says will happen. We're moving toward a one-world government in which one man will arise who will dominate all mankind.

Signs of the Times

Recently there's been a great deal of concern about the ozone blanket around the earth. Ozone is a form of oxygen. Oxygen has two atoms to the molecule, and ozone has three atoms to the molecule. The third atom easily escapes and combines with others, making ozone an excellent cleaning compound. The earth is surrounded with a blanket of ozone gas in the stratosphere. This layer of gas plays a very important part in man's survival by acting as a filter and protecting us from bombardment by the sun's lethal ultraviolet rays. In the book of Job, God mentions a "swaddling-band" around the earth.[3] This may have been a reference to the ozone layer that surrounds our planet. If the ozone layer were brought down to the earth's surface, it would form a blanket only three feet thick.

Our scientists are now saying that we're in danger of destroying this protective layer. Aerosol products release fluorocarbon gases into the air which cause the ozone to combine with nitrogen gas to form nitric oxide. Unless we change the gas within the aerosol cans (which has been done in the United States but not the rest of the world), we will continue to eradicate the ozone blanket.

The new supersonic jets that fly 1500 miles an hour at 55,000 feet also pose a threat to the ozone blanket. The gases emitted through the exhausts of these supersonic jets combine with oxygen and react with the ozone, diminishing the protective shield against the ultraviolet rays.

We are already beginning to observe the effects of this depleted ozone shield. I was baptizing several hundred people in the ocean recently, and as the result of several hours of exposure in the sun during this service, I received severe burns on my head. My doctor informed me they were ultraviolet burns which are becoming quite common because of ozone depletion.

In addition, the testing of atomic bombs releases great clouds of gases into the atmosphere which are detrimental to the existing ozone blanket. If we were to have an atomic war with a number of nuclear devices detonated within the atmosphere, the worst effect wouldn't necessarily be the initial destruction. It could very well be the destruction of the ozone layer. Without this blanket, the ultraviolet rays of the sun would begin to cook people alive.

In Revelation 16 we read that when the fourth vial is poured out by the angel during the Great Tribulation, power is given unto the sun to scorch men with fire.[4] This could very well be a description of ultraviolet radiation effects as the result of the disappearing ozone layer. This calamity was predicted 2,000 years ago, before anyone even knew that a protective ozone blanket existed in our atmosphere.

Scientists estimate that unless we take immediate and radical steps to reverse the deterioration of the ozone blanket, we could deplete it within ten years, and the ultraviolet rays of the sun would, in fact, scorch men upon the earth. Scientists are saying, "Reverse direction, or it's the end of the world!" That's not much different from that traditional picture of the old man with the sandwich board who says, "Repent. The end is near!"

Besides destroying the ozone layer, man is also guilty of harming our environment by recklessly using chemicals to control pests. The only way the world can produce enough crops to keep us all from starving to death is through the use of massive amounts of pesticides. But we don't fully know the consequences and side effects of these chemicals on our health, lives, or future. In years past one of the most prominent insecticides in widespread use was DDT. Now DDT has been banned in the United States, but not in the other parts of the world. We have discovered that DDT doesn't disintegrate in the soil but remains in its same chemical form. When it rains DDT flows into the streams. From the streams this insecticide flows into the rivers and then into the oceans. We are now beginning to discover the tremendous effect DDT has on the marine environment. It destroys seaweed, microscopic plant and animal life, and fish. Many thriving fishing businesses on the California coast have had to close down as a result of DDT contamination. It's estimated that perhaps only one-tenth of the DDT previously used has reached the oceans as yet. We don't know what will happen when the other nine-tenths get there.

The fact that we can destroy a major portion of the life within the ocean also coincides with another plague spoken of in the book of Revelation. John saw a great mountain burning with fire fall into the sea, and the third part of the creatures living within the sea were destroyed.[5]

We are also being warned about overpopulation. Experts predict that unless something dramatic is done to curb the spiral of population growth, by the year 2000 the earth will be wall-to-wall with people. The earth's population has already risen to over 6 billion people, and continues to grow at the rate of 2 percent of the total population each year. Even now we cannot feed all the people on the planet. The majority today go to bed hungry and undernourished. As the population increases, the demand for food increases, but the supply of food decreases. And so we see food prices rising sky-high.

Jesus said that famine would be one of the signs of the end of the world.[6] Revelation tells of a time that is coming when a "measure of wheat" (roughly a quart) will be sold for a day's wage (approximately $30 dollars).[7]

If you are planning to be around for this coming catastrophe and want to "hedge your bets," don't invest your money in silver or gold. Put it in wheat. What good will your gold be if you can't buy anything with it? In fact, James warns of the last days, "Go to now, ye rich men, weep and howl for your miseries that shall come upon you.... Your gold and silver is cankered."[8]

Man has also created a new generation of incredibly devastating weapons. It is estimated that the nuclear arsenal of the United States now amounts to a destructive capability the equivalent of 15 tons of TNT for every person alive on the earth.

In speaking of the end of the world, Jesus said, "Except those days should be shortened, there should no flesh be saved."[9] For centuries the idea that man could completely destroy himself was be considered preposterous. But now we have enough explosive power to destroy every man, woman, and child living on the planet 15 times over. Our military men are warning us that a major nuclear war could easily mean the end of the world.

Along with this our energy resources are rapidly being depleted. We used to take oil out of the ground as if there were no tomorrow. We thought we certainly had enough energy reserves to last for the foreseeable future. Now we are constantly being asked to curb our normal use of energy until science can discover some alternate resource. Our fossil-fuel reserves are limited, and scientists predict the approaching end for this type of energy.

Earthquakes are increasing in frequency and intensity around the earth. This is another striking sign that Jesus said would signal the time of His return.[10] Physicists are also getting into the act of prophesying doom. In studying the earth's structure, they find that the ions affected by the earth's magnetism are lined up differently from what is now true north. Some scientists believe this is the result of a polar axis shift. According to some researchers, these shifts occur approximately every

5,000 years. It has been speculated that the last polar axis shift coincided with the flood of Noah's time. This could well mean that we're overdue for another major shift. Some scientists believe that during a polar axis shift, islands disappear, mountains melt into valleys, and ocean floors become land masses. The whole area of Utah used to be a vast ocean. There are ocean shell fossils at 7,000 feet above sea level on the south rim of the Grand Canyon, indicating a major change in the oceans and the mountain structures from the past. Such changes supposedly happened during the last polar axis shift. It is impossible to calculate the geological damage that will result from such an upheaval of nature.

When we read passages that describe an event where "every mountain and island were moved out of their places,"[11] and "the earth shall stagger like a drunken man and shall be moved out of her place,"[12] it's easy to wonder if God is possibly foretelling a polar axis shift.

Creation and Termination

It used to be considered scientifically naive to talk about a specific time of creation, but physicists are now realizing that there must have been such a day. Sir James Jeans in his book *The Universe Around Us* says that the universe is like a giant clock that was wound up and is slowly running down. A prime example of the evidence that points to a specific starting point in time for our universe is found in our own sun. In order to give off the vast amount of energy that allows for our survival on planet Earth, the sun must consume over 2 million tons of its own mass every second. This creates a huge problem if the universe has existed from eternity past. Over such a huge stretch of time, not only our sun, but every sun in the entire universe would have burned out its fuel supply billions of years ago. A star with enough mass to burn literally forever would have to be as large as the universe itself. Therefore, it is now commonly acceptable to look back to a specific point in time called the day of creation. However, scientists are now looking to the future at a much more disturbing point of time called "the day of termination."

Social scientists are concerned, not so much about the physical aspects of the planet as much as with the behavior of the men upon it. Many experts are questioning the possibility of human survival even if we manage to avoid a physical catastrophe. They are alarmed at the rising increase in social hostility. Police departments and law enforcement agencies are confessing their inability to cope with the sheer number of crimes they attempt to handle.

Have you called a policeman lately? If you are the victim of a crime, the police will come out and make a report, but they give very little encouragement about recovering anything stolen or missing. If a child has run away, they will file a missing person's report. But there's very little promise of a happy ending to the crisis. So much crime exists that many experts have actually given up any hope of establishing law and order.

Paul wrote to Timothy, "In the last days perilous times shall come. For men shall be . . . without natural affection, truce breakers . . . incontinent, fierce, lovers of pleasures more than lovers of God."[13] Sadly, the Bible describes men as we see them today.

How ironic that with all the scientists, the professors, the militarists, and the sociologists crying, "The end of the world!" the Church has been so silent. It may be that the Church is so preoccupied with its dwindling attendance rolls and increased financial burdens that it hasn't noticed the signs of the times.

Perhaps another cause is that people in the past have foolishly and unscripturally set dates for the return of Christ even though Jesus said, "No man knows the day or the hour."[14] Many people have come and gone, proclaiming a special revelation of the specific time of the second advent. Perhaps because of the embarrassment caused by these unfortunate predictions, the Church has shunned the field of prophecy.

When the disciples asked, "What will be the sign of the end of the world?" Jesus didn't say, "It's none of your business!" He went into great detail to describe the signs preceding the time of the end.[15]

The Real New World

When Christians speak of the world and its end, we are talking about something entirely different than the scientists. The secular expert is talking about the end of the world in a physical sense. But when Christians talk about the end of the world, we are speaking of a set and ordered system that rejects God. The world order around us that is governed by Satan in rebellion against God is coming to a final and conclusive end.

Man has tried just about every form of government that can be conceived in the human mind. City-states, monarchies, democracies, dictatorships, and various forms of socialism have all been tried with varying degrees of success and failure. Man has attempted many different ways to govern himself, but every form of government has ultimately deteriorated. No matter how theoretically perfect the system, man cannot rule himself without greed and corruption setting in. Most forms of government have been able to endure for only about 200 years before totally disintegrating.

We, the Church, look for a new form of government: a monarchy that will embrace the entire world and endure forever. We're waiting for the kingdom of God to come when righteousness will cover the earth as the waters cover the sea.

We do not know the day or the hour when this perfect kingdom will come, but Jesus said, "Watch therefore . . . be ye also ready, for in such an hour as ye think not the Son of man cometh."[16] Christ then presented a series of parables by which He illustrated the importance of watching and being ready for His return to receive His Church unto Himself.

The Church has great cause to cry, "The end of the world!" So many signs of the end have already been fulfilled. For instance God has established His nation Israel back in its historic homeland as He promised through the prophets. Ezekiel tells us that Israel would no longer be two nations (which was the case when it divided into northern and southern kingdoms in the tenth century B.C.), but it would become one nation upon the land, and one king would rule over the people.[17] God also said that Israel would again build the waste places and "they that come from Jacob shall blossom and bud and fill the face of the world with fruit."[18]

How interesting that Israel is now the fourth largest exporter of fruit to the world. That is an amazing fact when you realize that this tiny nation is about the size of the state of New Jersey. Israel is also the main supplier of flowers throughout all of Europe. Because of Israel's good climate and favorable growing conditions, flower growing has become one of the country's major industries.

God has fulfilled His promise to bring Israel back together and to cause the Jewish people to prosper in the land. But also, as the Bible predicted, it seems that now Israel is standing almost alone against all the nations of the earth. Yet God has promised that He would stand beside them, even though all the nations of the earth gather together against them.[19]

The author of Psalm 102 states, "When the Lord shall build up Zion, he shall appear in his glory."[20] Zion (the nation of Israel) is being built up; the time has come for the Lord to appear in His glory. Christ first came to earth to be crucified. He came as a humble servant as the prophets predicted. "Behold, thy King cometh unto thee; lowly, and riding upon an ass, and upon a colt the foal of an ass."[21] But Jesus is coming a second time not as a suffering teacher of truth, but with great power and glory![22] When the psalmist said, "When the Lord shall build up Zion then shall He also appear in His glory," he was referring to the Second Coming. The Church ought to be crying, "The end of the world!" because God is now building up Zion, the land of Israel. We see in the world today the famines, earthquakes, and pestilences Christ foretold. Doctors are always warning us of new flu strains that are worse than those we've had so far. Staph infections and other viruses are becoming more and more immune to antibiotics. Add to these the awesome threat of the AIDS virus.

It seems that there is no way out of the economic, social, or universal problems confronting us today. As we look at the nations, there is no dominant power in the world today. The world is divided and the nations are in perplexity. Even the experts don't know what to do about the economic situation, the energy crisis, or increasing food shortages. There are perplexities of nations just as the Scripture said would take place in the end times.[23]

Men are looking for a leader. A leader is coming, and they'll be drawn to follow him. He's going to come in his own name, proclaiming marvelous things. He's going to have an incredibly efficient and universal economic program of computerized commerce.

Is it all just a coincidence? Or did God know what He was talking about when He spoke of these things 2,000 years ago! Jesus said, "When these things begin to come to pass, then look up, and lift up your heads, for your redemption draweth nigh."[24]

The Church ought to be looking up, looking for and expecting our Lord. We should be proclaiming: "The end of the world!"

This is not a cry of despair or of doom and gloom, for the end of this world system will mean an end of greed and hatred, wars and famines, sickness and death. The commercial exploitation of others, creating untold personal misery, will be gone forever. The prophet Isaiah called, "Ho! Everyone that is thirsty come to the water, and he that has no money let him buy and eat, come and buy wine and milk without money and without price, and let your soul delight itself in fatness."[25] The end of this world system will mark an end of the world governed by man in rebellion against God, and the beginning of a new world governed by God and marked by peace like a river.[26] A world where there is no pain or sorrow, "for God shall wipe away all tears."[27] We are told by Isaiah that the eyes of the blind shall be opened, and the ears of the deaf unstopped; the lame will leap like deer and the tongue of the mute shall sing.[28] He also tells us that men will beat their swords into plowshares and their spears into pruning hooks.[29] (That is, the military budgets will be diverted to agricultural development.) Last year, the nations of the world spent over $1 trillion in military expenditures. If this amount of money had been spent for agricultural development, not one person would have starved to death. The prophet Micah tells us, "Nation shall not lift up a sword against nation, neither shall they learn war any more. But they shall sit every man under his vine and under his fig tree, and none shall make them afraid."[30] That does not sound like doom and gloom to me, but like a beautiful ideal world where I desire to live. I have difficulty waiting for it to begin. "Even so, come quickly, Lord Jesus."[31]

Jesus shall reign as King of Kings and Lord of Lords. Ours is not a gloomy picture of desolation and destruction at the end of the world as the forecasting of scientists so often is. Ours is the glorious prediction of the end of this corrupted old world order of man. An end to rule by greed, an end to wars and hatred, and the beginning of the new world ruled by Jesus Christ where men will live together in peace and love. I long for this new world and pray daily, "Thy kingdom come, Thy will be done in earth, even as it is in heaven."

4

Escape

Our world is in a death-dive. We have peaked, and now we're plunging rapidly to the end. Moral rot and decay have so corrupted the planks of our society that they will soon crumble and fall. The only hope for escape is for Jesus Christ to snatch His followers out of this mad fatal plunge.

The rest of the world will have seven years before the end. The first 3½ years will be a period of unprecedented peace and prosperity. But during the second 3½ years, we'll see God's wrath poured out upon this earth. Jesus describes this judgment to come as a time of tribulation such as the world has never seen or will ever see again.[1]

So, how do you become a follower of Jesus Christ and escape the impending destruction?

God's Main Message

God's main message to us can be summed up in the word "repent." If we repent, then God will forgive us our sins. But what does it mean to repent? It doesn't mean just to be sorry, because you can be sorry for the things you've done and yet go right on doing them. To repent means to have a total change of heart and mind toward God. It means humbly turning away from the shallow and empty things in which you have tried to find fulfillment and turning toward the love and forgiveness of Jesus Christ. This change of heart towards God will give you the power to turn from your wrong and sinful lifestyles. When you experience the goodness of God, you will also experience a genuine desire to change from your sins of the past. You will experience a brand-new quality of life the Bible calls godliness.

In Revelation 9 we are given this frightful scenario; a terrible horde of 200,000,000 satanic creatures will be loosed from the area of the river Euphrates in Iraq to bring mass destruction upon the earth. By this insidious force, one-third of the world's population will be destroyed. The idea of a spiritually inspired invasion force becomes more significant in light of the fact that Islamic religious leaders, who can boast of 750,000,000 followers worldwide, are constantly threatening a Jihad (holy war) against their enemies, which they identify as the non-Islamic world in general and Israel in particular. Whatever its source, an incredible portrait of destruction is clearly predicted to come upon mankind.

Why?

Why will there be such awful judgment upon the earth? Why such horrible tribulation? Because people have been guilty of forsaking the laws of God. Sin has its own inevitable consequence: death.

God has revealed to us the way to a meaningful life. He says, "If you'll follow My rules, you'll be happy and prosperous."[2] But man has hardened his heart, rejected God, and gone after his own way. God describes the conditions in the world that this rejection brings, conditions that will bring judgment.

The Bible says that the people left on the earth in the last days "repented not of the works of their hands, that they should not worship devils, and idols . . . neither repented they of their murders, nor of their sorceries, nor of their fornication, nor of their thefts."[3]

This picture of the character of mankind is sobering to say the least. What will people be like at the time of the end? First of all, people will be worshiping devils. God wants us to seek His guidance and His wisdom. He wants to bring direction to our lives. But today people are not seeking the counsel of God. Instead they are turning to mediums and New Age channelers for guidance. They seek the advice of psychics, fortune tellers, Ouija boards, and horoscopes. They are worshiping devils rather than God.

The New Age Movement with its growing popularity has brought the phenomenon of "channeling," where supposed wise people of the past give their secrets and wisdom to present-day seekers. This is similar to the practices of the oracles of ancient times. In essence it is no more than demons promulgating their doctrines through mediums, dressed up and made acceptable to modern consumers.

In the public school system in the United States, children are taught how to contact their spirit guides and receive help from the wise little man who lives in a house in their mind.

Many of the popular rock groups are encouraging children to find fulfillment through Satanism. Clearly the prediction of widespread worship of demonic spirits is coming to pass.

Not only will they worship devils, but the people of the last days will also worship idols. Everyone bows his knee to some object of worship, some idea, some principle, some goal, some ambition, or some thing. Every man must worship; this is an innate need. If he doesn't worship God, then he must and will find a substitute. The Bible speaks of man literally being driven to worship. It is an inescapable part of our nature.

Many Christian college students are ridiculed by their secular professors because of their belief in Jesus Christ. Professors make Christians one of their favorite targets, mocking and laughing at those who believe in God. Students are told that man is self-sufficient, with no need for an outdated crutch like faith in God. But then the professor goes home and worships an idol in his backyard! Maybe it's a boat, a sports car, or a garden he's cultivating. Many of these same professors are using drugs or are involved in the New Age Movement. They flock to Sai Baba or other gurus who claim to have made the transition into the godhood. Every man has his idol.

Men in the last days will not repent of their murders and sorceries. In the abortion clinics of the United States today, condoned and in many cases financed by the government and defended by the courts, millions of babies are being murdered each year. God cannot ignore this wanton disregard for life and will surely bring the United States into judgment for it. Perhaps this judgment is already beginning. Once disorganized street gangs have now become well-financed and well-equipped purveyors of drugs and violence. We now find addiction and wanton, senseless murder becoming commonplace in every major city in America.

Scripture also tells us that the people of the last days will refuse to repent of their sorceries. "Sorceries" in the original Greek is *pharmakia*, which means "the use of narcotics for thrill or enchantment." Look at the increasingly widespread use of drugs throughout the world today. Marijuana and cocaine are as easily obtained by the youth as candy. These are both personality-changing drugs. The insidious thing about their use is the effect on the brain of the user. These drugs seem to attack the centers of rational judgment so that the user is deceived into believing he is not addicted. An objective observer can see the alteration of personality and loss of good judgment quite easily. The person who is under the influence cannot assess that he is making poor decisions. He hasn't the capability to realize that his ability to make rational choices has been impaired, and is thus trapped.

New research reveals that these drugs destroy a chemical in the brain that inhibits the ability to ever resist the drug again.

"Neither did they repent of their fornication." As we look around the world today, we see the lowering and ultimate eradication of any decent standard of morality. It seems that almost every mass medium of communication is being used to destroy the moral principles that our society and its people once possessed. Immorality has become so pervasive and accepted that people talk freely of their live-in partners as if the practice was beyond question.

One young lady who was about to get married went to a minister for counseling. The minister asked her, "Have you been living with your fiancé?"

She said, "Of course not!"

He replied, "How do you know whether or not you want to marry him? You should live with him for a few months." He then had the audacity to charge her $25 for his advice! This minister wears a robe and collar that distinguishes him as a clergyman. He's a minister all right, but not of Jesus Christ.

The Lord said that final judgment is coming for a variety of reasons. One is the condition of open fornication. It is difficult in this day and age, with all the pressure to the contrary from society, to keep pure. But the Word of God says that we must flee the fleshly lusts that war against men's souls.[4] God's laws have not changed. God's rules have not been altered. They're still the same today, and with good reason. God clearly sees the destruction, disease, and human misery that result from a life dedicated to hedonistic pleasure. People are precious to God. It breaks His heart to see the tremendous amount of suffering caused by fornication.

"Nor of their thefts." A young man was working on his doctorate in the science department of a famous university. He said that practically every bit of equipment in the science lab was stolen property. When he refused to do his project on stolen equipment, his fellow students laughed at him. They said he'd never complete his doctorate unless he was willing to steal some kind of equipment to perform his experiments.

We've come to a place where we easily justify thievery. Today it's very common to steal from the job. So-called "white collar" crime is reaching epidemic proportions. The rationale is often, "They're not paying me enough. I deserve more, so I'll supplement my income." We may see it as a small indiscretion, but God sees it as open sin. For these things comes the wrath of God upon the earth.

Perhaps the most shocking aspect of this prophecy is the reaction of the people who must endure this terror. In spite of the invasion of the demonic horde and the fact that one-third of all people on earth are massacred, the two-thirds that remain do not repent of their sins. It makes one wonder just what it takes to bring a man to repentance, to turn him from his sins and back to God. Rarely do judgments bring a person to repentance. As a general rule, judgment only hardens an individual's heart against God, as it did with the case of Pharaoh in the story of Moses.

It is the goodness of God that brings a man to repentance.[5] Though so many of us have been guilty of worshiping devils, guilty of having idols, guilty of murder, drugs, fornication, or thievery, God still loves us. He loves us so much that He sent His only begotten Son to take the responsibility of the guilt of every wrong thing that we have ever done. Jesus Christ died on the cross in our place so that He could wash us clean from guilt forever.

But so many say, "I'll wait until I see God's judgments come upon this earth; then I'll turn to God for mercy." Allow me to speak to you personally. If you don't repent now as the result of the goodness and mercy of God, why would you repent during the time of God's judgments? If the goodness of God doesn't bring you into His family, His judgments are not likely to do it.

Repentance must be the work of God within your life. No person can bring you to repentance. Someone might bring you to sorrow. I might make you feel very sorry, but I can't make you repent. You must allow God to speak to you and touch your heart. Only godly sorrow leads to repentance.

Stop and reflect. Whatever you may be getting out of your experiences of worshiping devils or idols, committing fornication, or taking drugs, is it worth the sacrifice of your soul? Why not turn your life over to Jesus Christ? He has a much better plan for your life today and a glorious eternal future in His kingdom tomorrow! What true profit is it if you gain the whole world but lose your own soul?

Take a moment in the quiet of your heart to give your life to Jesus. Acknowledge the fact that Jesus, God in human flesh, died on the cross for your sins. Humbly ask Him for the forgiveness and eternal life He so freely offers. This is the only way to know that all will be well with you at the final curtain.

Notes

Introduction and Chapter 1

1. Matthew 24:36
2. 1 Thessalonians 5:1,2,4
3. Daniel 2:47
4. Daniel 3:25,27
5. Revelation 13:15
6. Revelation 7:1-8
7. Daniel 4:31-37
8. Daniel 7:1-8
9. 2 Thessalonians 2:3,4
10. Revelation 13:4,16,17
11. Zechariah 11:17
12. Matthew 24:15
13. Daniel 9:22-24
14. Daniel 9:25,26
15. 2 Chronicles 36:22,23
16. Luke 19:42
17. Daniel 9:26,27
18. Matthew 24:15-18
19. 2 Thessalonians 2:4
20. Isaiah 45:1
21. Jeremiah 50:9
22. Jeremiah 50:13
23. Jeremiah 50:26
24. Luke 21:26
25. Genesis 18:25
26. Genesis 18:32
27. 2 Peter 2:9
28. 1 Thessalonians 5:9
29. 1 Thessalonians 4:15-18
30. Luke 21:25
31. Isaiah 13:6
32. Revelation 13:17
33. 2 Thessalonians 2:1,2
34. 2 Thessalonians 2:3
35. 2 Thessalonians 2:7-10

36. John 3:16
37. Matthew 24:15, 2 Thessalonians 2:3,4
38. 2 Peter 3:11
39. Hebrews 12:25-27
40. Luke 19:13

Chapter 2

1. Daniel 9:24-26
2. John 5:43
3. "Let's See Your I.D." *Herald Examiner*, 22 January 1977, p. 1.
4. Ezekiel 37:14
5. Ezekiel 38:10
6. Ezekiel 38:6
7. Ezekiel 38:4
8. Ezekiel 38:18
9. Ezekiel 39:27-29
10. Ezekiel 10:18,19
11. Romans 11:25
12. Zechariah 12:8
13. Judges 16:26-30
14. 1 Corinthians 15:51,52
15. John R. Hersey, *Hiroshima* (New York: Random House, Inc., 1946), p. 68
16. Zechariah 12:2-9
17. Zechariah 14:12
18. Luke 21:28

Chapter 3

1. Lewis W. Walt, *The Eleventh Hour* (Otta, IL: Carline House Publishers)
2. Ibid.
3. Job 38:9
4. Revelation 9:20,21
5. Revelation 8:10
6. Matthew 24:7
7. Revelation 6:6
8. James 5:1-3
9. Matthew 24:22
10. Matthew 24:7
11. Revelation 6:14
12. Isaiah 24:20
13. 2 Timothy 3:1-4

14. Mark 13:32
15. Matthew 24:3-14
16. Matthew 25:13
17. Ezekiel 37:22
18. Isaiah 27:6
19. Zechariah 12:3
20. Psalm 102:6
21. Zechariah 9:9
22. Matthew 24:30
23. Luke 21:25
24. Luke 21:28
25. Isaiah 55:2
26. Isaiah 66:12
27. Revelation 21:4
28. Isaiah 35:6
29. Isaiah 2:4
30. Micah 4:3,4
31. Revelation 22:20

Chapter 4

1. Matthew 24:21
2. Deuteronomy 30:15,16
3. Revelation 9:21
4. 1 Peter 2:11
5. Romans 2:4

BOOKS BY CHUCK SMITH

Dateline Earth: Countdown to Eternity—What lies ahead for our planet? Startling, up-to-date answers from the book of Revelation. (Hardbound)

Charisma vs. Charismania—A balanced biblical perspective on the person and ministry of the Holy Spirit today.

The Gospel According to Grace—Is Christianity a religion or a relationship? Clear answers from the book of Romans.

The Tribulation and the Church—An unprecedented time of God's judgment is fast approaching. Will Christians experience this?

What the World Is Coming To—A complete commentary on the book of Revelation . . . and the scenario for the last days.

Harvest—The exciting story of God choosing and using the most unlikely people to share His love. Pastors from ten Calvary Chapels share how God broke through such barriers as fear, drug dependency, pride, and complacency to carry out His plan for this vital ministry.

Effective Prayer Life—Biblical principles that can transform prayer from the realm of obligation to a full, beautiful experience.

The Answer for Today, vol. 1—Can Christians be demon-possessed? Does the God who made everything have time for me? Can I get anything I want from God simply by claiming His promises in faith? On-target, biblical responses to ten of today's toughest questions.

The Answer for Today, vol. 2—What is the proper motive for serving God? Can God use even physical suffering for good in our lives? Is there proof that the Bible is the Word of God? More powerful insights from the teaching ministry of Pastor Chuck Smith.